Lives in Cricket: No 47

Brian Sellers
Yorkshire Tyrant

Mark Rowe

First published in Great Britain by
Association of Cricket Statisticians and Historians
Cardiff CF11 9XR.
© ACS, 2017

Mark Rowe has asserted his right under the Copyright, Designs
and Patents Act 1988 to be identified as the author of this work.

All Rights Reserved. No part of this publication may be reproduced, stored in
a retrieval system, or transmitted in any form, or by any means, electronic,
mechanical, photocopying, recording or otherwise without the prior permission
in writing of the Copyright holders, nor be otherwise circulated in any form, or
binding or cover other than in which it is published and without a similar condition
including this condition being imposed on the subsequent publisher.

British Library Cataloguing-in-Publication Data.
A catalogue record for this book is available from the British Library.

ISBN: 978 1 908165 82 4
Typeset and printed by The City Press Leeds Ltd

Contents

Chapter One	Oxford, May 1932	5
Chapter Two	Sellers and son	12
Chapter Three	The line that disciplines the fell	23
Chapter Four	On the field	37
Chapter Five	Off the field	54
Chapter Six	Batsman, fielder, bowler – and England captain?	62
Chapter Seven	Wartime	75
Interlude	Two team photographs	80
Chapter Eight	Treachery in Australia 1946/47	83
Chapter Nine	Last seasons 1946-48	91
Chapter Ten	The Wardle Affair	102
Chapter Eleven	The Sixties	109
Chapter Twelve	When I'm 64: Illingworth and Close	119
Chapter Thirteen	Keighley, December 2015	133
Thanks and sources		148
Appendix	Some Statistics	151
Index		153

Chapter One
Oxford, May 1932

Strolling along the banks of Isis and Cherwell on a summer afternoon, watching the white-clad figures of young athletes playing cricket on the lawns of the University Parks, or the punts proceeding at a leisurely pace along the Thames, one comes closer to the peculiar idea of an English Arcadia, to the English conception of happiness.
ZA Grabowski, Your Undiscovered Island (1950)

The newspapers agreed that the match between Yorkshire and Oxford University was nothing out of the ordinary. The newspapers were wrong. They did not report anything wrongly; rather, as so often, they missed the most important event, that would define Yorkshire county cricket for the next five decades.

It happened out of sight, on the second day, Thursday 5 May. Ever since a storm had broken over Oxford and district on the previous Sunday afternoon, that flooded some roads, it had been no weather for cricket. Fred Harvey, The Parks groundsman, was able to remove some of the water from the pitch on the Tuesday evening, and it did not rain on Wednesday; even so, play only began at 3.40 pm. The new captain of Yorkshire, Brian Sellers, won the toss, and chose to bat. The famous opening pair of Percy Holmes and Herbert Sutcliffe had to watch the ball that sometimes 'kicked'. Yorkshire closed the day on 170 for three.

In some years, when the county traditionally began its season there, batsmen could walk to the middle in shirt sleeves. In 1936 the anonymous *Bradford Telegraph and Argus* reporter said: 'Every time I come to this lovely park ground I am amazed at the number of shades of green .... in the trees which surround it .... Flowers, sunshine and soft spring breezes too all help to make a perfect setting.' It did not feel like that in 1932, under grey skies, in the keen north-east wind – from Yorkshire, indeed. *The Cricketer* magazine's Oxford correspondent, Isis, called it 'the coldest day upon which the writer remembers ever to have watched a cricket match'.

On that second, brighter, day, 'Sellars' – so mistyped by the *Oxford Mail* – went in to bat next after Holmes was out for 110. Alan Melville the Varsity captain had just brought on his leg spinner, Tuppy Owen-Smith, 'and the Yorkshire captain did not shape at all well at his first over', the *Oxford Mail* reported. However, Sellers got going, and Melville brought himself on instead of Owen-Smith. 'The Keighley amateur,' said the *Yorkshire Evening News*, meaning Sellers, 'made good use of the full drive and this stroke

5

brought him two fours without any effort at all.' Two more wickets fell and Sellers declared, himself 18 not out, and Yorkshire 229 for six.

George Macaulay and Hedley Verity opened the bowling, and Maurice Leyland took over from Verity. The event came before Leyland took the first wicket, well caught wide on the leg side by wicket-keeper Arthur Wood, from the last ball before lunch. It came before or after Arthur Mitchell was twice hit when fielding close, 'the second blow being above the knee of the leg which was so badly damaged last season. He went off for attention by Bright Heyhirst, the Leeds rugby league club trainer,' the *Yorkshire Evening News* told readers that night. So far, so usual for Yorkshire, whose aggressive bowling and fielding – though dangerous – were already proving too much for the students.

Brian Sellers, on his debut for the first team, had already had to wait hours before he could do a thing. Unexpectedly and suddenly, he faced what he later called 'the only nasty moment I ever had as skipper':

It was a lovely day, very hot. George Macaulay opened the bowling very well. At the end of his sixth or seventh over he put his sweater on and I saw that and I thought, 'Hello, there's something going on here.' At the end of the following over Mac said, 'Where do you want me to field, skipper?' I said I didn't realise I'd asked you to end your spell – there's only one gaffer here and you'll carry on until luncheon for a two-hour spell if you drop down.' This worried me all morning. What do I do? I thought, well, better the day, better the deed. In the dressing room after lunch I told them all, 'Mac tried to take a rise out of me. I'm a rookie and I'm relying on you, but my decision is final. I know I'm not in the same class as you as a batter or bowler – my dad has made that clear to me – he says I shouldn't be associated with you, that I shouldn't be spoken in the same breath as you. But I can hold my place in the field with any of you. And you Mac,' I said to George Macaulay, 'you're being clever. You're taking a rise out of me – and I tell you what – you've bowled all bloody morning and you're starting again after lunch. And he did. Never any trouble.

A couple of details are, frankly, inaccurate. If that early May day did turn hot, that was probably only later in the afternoon. Sellers gave the impression that Yorkshire were in the field all morning, making it more of a punishment to keep Macaulay bowling. In fact Sellers had left Oxford 40 minutes' batting before lunch. None of the reports suggested Macaulay bowled for a strangely long time, though he did bowl the most overs – 18 – of anyone in Oxford's 56-over first innings. By contrast in the second, Macaulay bowled least of the five bowlers. While our memories can trick us, Macaulay – 'an awkward so-and-so', in the words of sketch-writer and later Yorkshire MP J.P.W.Mallalieu – had evidently tried to treat Sellers as captain in name only. Sellers had seen it and stamped on it.

Not long before Oxford were all out 74 behind, Sellers made a run-out thanks to what the *Yorkshire Post* called a 'fine throw from extra cover'. Yorkshire closed the second day on 100 for six. Sellers had promoted himself only to be leg before to Owen-Smith for one. The Friday, the final day, dawned with frost on the grass and ice on standing water. Yorkshire set Oxford 282; the students folded for 119. Sellers gave the longest bowls to the other two colts on debut, Frank Smailes and Arthur Rhodes. The reporters had more to say about them (Smailes took five wickets in the second innings; Rhodes was no relation to Wilfred) than the new captain, whether because Sellers did less, or it did not do to judge the county captain; or, they saw Sellers as simply the latest amateur – the seventh since the 1914-18 war – passing through as captain for a season or two. If they ever heard of the confrontation, first in the middle (that strange place, at the same time in public view and out of earshot) and then in the dressing room, they never reported it. R.C.Robertson-Glasgow once hinted at it, or – as impressive – guessed it. 'But his first victory, which did not receive the notice of print, was the greatest, the showing that he was to be captain in fact as well as in name,' 'Crusoe' wrote in a sketch published in 1941. 'The medicine was bitter to some; they swallowed it, and felt better. He stood no nonsense, and was liked.'

Rain ruined Yorkshire's next two matches, against MCC, and Cambridge University. At Lord's Sellers was out again to a slow bowler – bowled by Jack Hearne for five. The *London Evening Standard* reckoned he 'stayed long enough to enable critics to form a favourable impression of his style'. Even if he did impress, Yorkshire did not make Sellers captain for his

An intriguing 1932, presumably pre-season, team picture beside the bowling green at Headingley.
Standing(l to r): Arthur Wood, Frank Dennis, Arthur Rhodes, Bill Bowes, Hedley Verity, Arthur Mitchell, Wilf Barber, William Ringrose (Scorer).
Seated: George Macauley, Percy Holmes, Brian Sellers, Frank Greenwood, Herbert Sutcliffe, Maurice Leyland. Judging by his rather cramped body – compared with Greenwood's – the cravat-wearing Sellers looks a man not yet settled on his image as a Yorkshire captain, not at ease among those men, despite his county blazer. No wonder, if he had yet to take the field for the first team!?

style. If he lasted, it would only be because he impressed his men – who paradoxically were of a better 'class' than him (as Sellers had been quick to admit). And yet because they were professionals, paid players, who belonged to a lower social class, their county would not trust any of them to be captain. Sellers had to do more than win cricket matches; he had to win over men.

Sellers had seen the trap. If he had allowed the most senior players to control who bowled when, he would never have retrieved the lost power. Other followers of English cricket understood the amateur captain's plight, because every county was the same. Sellers' first opposing captain, Alan Melville went on to Sussex. When he told the club at the end of the 1934 season he could no longer captain them, the *Sussex Daily News* commented:

The qualities of a good captain are many. He must be more than a good cricketer. He must have that genius of the heart which wins the friendship of the players. And yet it must be tempered with that sense of discipline which exacts the highest effort.

A good captain had to be chummy – and not. The Ashbourne journalist 'Plaindealer' writing in 1930 in praise of Derbyshire's 1920s captain G.R.Jackson, recalled how through binoculars he once saw a fielder talk to Jackson in a way that Plaindealer took as an 'act of insubordination'. The player might have thought himself indispensable; 'he found he was wrong'. According to *Plaindealer*, Guy Jackson 'approached the ideal of a county skipper':

The post has always demanded determination, tact, personality, good judgement and equable temperament and the power of exercising discipline from its occupant. These have been essential apart from a captain's abilities as a cricketer, and it has always been desirable that the office holder should be able to play 'a captain's innings' on occasion and a column might easily be filled before the subject of what was required of a skipper was exhausted.

Significantly, *Plaindealer* went on to what Jackson was not:

There have been since the war more county captains than one who have not been captains save in name. They have done what their committees have wished or their senior professionals have told them to do. The true story of how one famous pro' came to the front of the players' balcony at Lord's, of all places in the world, and clapped his hands to signify to his captain who was batting in the middle that it was time that the innings was declared, is typical of these well-meaning captains who have possibly accepted office from a sense of duty and done their best.

As that suggested, having a good nature – in Sellers' case, if he had welcomed Macaulay for making his life easier - made you a weak captain. While we have no way of knowing, that story of *Plaindealer*'s may have been of Yorkshire; Wilfred Rhodes notoriously told his 1920s captains what to do. Like Caesar, the wise county captain never dropped his guard in case of assassins. To captain the likes of Wilfred Rhodes, you had to be as knowledgeable as them, or at least seek knowledge – and always keeping a balance between respecting the players for knowing more than you, and not letting them boss you about.

To hope to excel, you had to devote yourself to such learning; unlike Surrey's 1920s captain, Percy Fender, who according to the sports writer Herbert Henley could 'detach himself completely from the game ... and live an intellectually different life'. Henley gave the example of Fender sitting in the writing room of The Oval pavilion, dictating business letters to a clerk, at a critical stage of a match. When a wicket fell, Fender rose, and five minutes later 'he was hitting fours off Macaulay and Rhodes'. Henley admired Fender for having more to his life than cricket; however, under Fender, Surrey did no better than come second – once to Yorkshire.

In Sellers' first years as captain, Sussex challenged Yorkshire most, coming second from 1932 to 1934. Each time it fell short, the county blamed injuries, tiring players, or not enough reserves – an 'extraordinary run of troubles' as the *Sussex Daily News* put it in its review of the 1935 season. It singled out Yorkshire and Lancashire (winners in 1934) as counties with 'unrivalled resources .... lots of players on the staff, quite enough to fill a gap in the first eleven at any time'. Sussex did not run a second team. Yorkshire's Second Eleven cost about £1000 a year, as much as three players' wages, 'money well spent' as the club's cricket committee chairman Arthur Sellers – Brian's father – told the 1935 annual general meeting.

While Sussex had a point – metropolitan counties that host Test matches have always had more to spend – were they making excuses? And did that explain why Yorkshire, and not Lancashire, under Sellers from 1932 won the Championship six summers in eight – a rare run in any sport? At the time, how Yorkshire kept doing it was the talk of English cricket; 'the marvel of the Yorkshire spirit', as Hampshire clubmen put it in the pavilion at Bournemouth when Yorkshire visited in July 1933. Sellers was not the sole reason; and yet such success in his time was no coincidence. His style of captaincy, the culture of the team, and the running of the

Yorkshire opening batsman Percy Holmes.

Hedley Verity.

Surrey captain Percy Fender.

club, off the field; all affected each other – as they do in any group of men, sporting and otherwise, in good years and bad.

Success soon came to Sellers; but not easily.

*Being skipper at the start – well, you see it was not very pleasant. One had to get to know the players. I'd met them, rather seen them when we'd been at the Headingley nets together, but nothing more than that. So I **had** to get to know them. I was the only amateur and stayed at my own hotel. The pro's were always frugal; they knew the good cheap places, the great little pubs and the pubs and hotels looked up the fixture lists and booked their regulars up a year ahead. I didn't like the idea much, being on my own. In the first match, at Oxford, I stayed at the Mitre, but on coming away from The Parks Maurice Leyland said to me, 'I don't know what you're doing tonight but you can join us if you like.' I hadn't liked to intrude, but they made me one of the circus.*

As Sellers added, comradeship developed. Note, though, that Sellers did not feel he could invite himself. As significant, the invitation came from Leyland, a senior player, but not as senior as Sutcliffe; although the rest of the team must have agreed first.

Sellers took time to find the right voice. In old age Fred Trueman told how, according to 'old players', Sellers in his early days might say 'my father says', and Macaulay once replied: 'Here's t'ball then. Get your dad to come and bowl these bastards out.'

Once he had settled, Sellers could make a joke – and let the whole county in on it. Responding to one of the toasts at the dinner in Pudsey in October 1938 to mark Len Hutton's record 364 for England, Sellers told the gathering of 300: 'I am very proud of the team; that is something that will live in my mind forever. There are times when I have got up their backs.'

The Surrey team 1934.

('Laughter,' the *Yorkshire Post* reported.) 'I know it. And I can tell you that they know it as well.' ('Loud laughter.') 'But we have played as 11 men. Because of that we have the honour of being champion county today.'

What Sellers' players made of that, they kept to themselves; at least at the time. John Arlott, in his old age, recalled how a conversation with Maurice Leyland turned to county captains. 'Nay, I don't count captain in t'Yorkshire side,' said Maurice. 'We do it with ten.'

To explain why the likes of Leyland accepted Sellers so grudgingly – and yet played under him as champions, year after year – we may as well start with where Sellers came from. For in Sellers' case, as in many others, players of an earlier generation had marked him, just as he would mark players of the next generation or two.

Chapter Two
Sellers and son

It is a safe thing to say that in no part of England is a greater interest taken in cricket, and nowhere is it followed with a keener critical appreciation than in Yorkshire.
JS Fletcher, Picturesque History of Yorkshire
in six volumes, volume V (1900)

When Brian Sellers began for Yorkshire, some still remembered his father, such as a *Nottingham Evening News* reporter in July 1932, 'and I was glad to learn he is still hale and hearty and follows the fortunes of his old team with unwavering interest'. Just as Sellers' playing years took in the Edwardians Jack Hearne and Frank Woolley, and after the 1939-45 war Derek Shackleton and Tom Graveney who played into the 1960s, through his father Sellers connected to great Victorian names.

His father was not quite one of them. In his 1924 memoirs, Yorkshire's famous captain Lord Hawke called Arthur Sellars (sic) 'a batsman whose career was all too short'. Arthur's story began, at least in the records, on 26 April 1887, at a Tuesday evening committee meeting of Keighley Cricket Club in the long-gone Devonshire Hotel. Arthur, not quite 17, was one of seven new members elected. At the annual general meeting in November, Arthur was among 11 voted on to the committee; and in February 1888, appointed as one of the two joint secretaries. Arthur began the 1887 season opening the batting for the second team. By June – in front of 2000 spectators at Burnley – after the hosts made 320, leaving Keighley one hour to bat, Sellers went in after three wickets soon fell. With the professional Tom Jeeves he nearly saw out time. A fortnight later Arthur was top scorer with 29 not out of 90 for eight at Dewsbury. When in May 1888 Arthur again top scored with a 'plucky and invaluable' 27 out of 70 as Keighley beat local rivals Saltaire, the weekly *Keighley News* - while noting an 'occasional tendency to hit out rashly' - praised him for 'fulfilling the predictions of those who last season nominated him as 'the coming man''. Days later Arthur batted and bowled as one of 22 colts that lost by an innings at Sheffield to the full Yorkshire side, including such Victorian names as Bobby Peel, George Ulyett and Lord Hawke. Arthur first played for Yorkshire in 1889 and most regularly in 1893, when he made two of the county's three centuries and scored 1062 runs. Occasionally he captained the county; only, the family business took him away. He was rather, as his obituary in the *Keighley News* put it, a Saturday club cricket 'giant', 'the idol of the crowd'. He made a record 11,779 runs for Keighley, and eight centuries, when hundreds in northern club cricket were rare. On his death in 1941 his 'flashing bat, his flashing bat, his unceremonious treatment of good bowling and his rapid scoring were things to remember'.

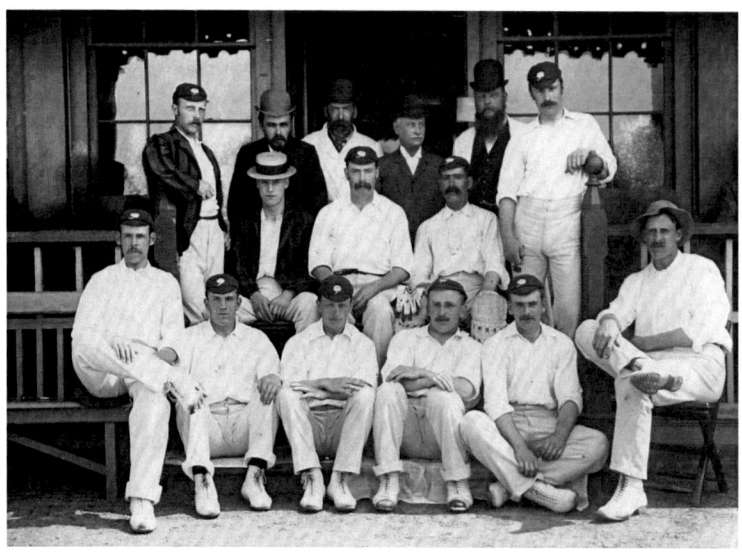

Yorkshire in 1893, county champions that season.
Arthur Sellers is seated, wearing the boater.

The Yorkshire team of 1905.
Lord Hawke, physically and symbolically, was central.
Back row (l to r): Charles Grimshaw, William Wilkinson, Wilfred Rhodes, David Hunter, Hubert Myers. Seated: George Hirst, Hon FS Jackson, Lord Hawke, Henry Wilkinson, John Tunnicliffe. Front: David Denton, Schofield Haigh.

Even in his playing days, Arthur gave time to the running of the game. He was a long-time county club committee man for Craven district; he attended the first meeting of the Yorkshire Cricket Council in Leeds in 1900. Just as his son followed that example, so Arthur was following his father, the founder of the family fortune. Robert Sellers was born in 1830 at Wyke, south of Bradford. He served an apprenticeship in a factory where his uncle was manager. Robert came to Keighley for the funeral of one of three Leeds men who had started a business in the town. Another of the three, William Darling, who had worked with Robert, persuaded him to become a partner of the firm in 1851. The men set up their tool-making works at Lawkholme, the part of town where the rugby league and cricket grounds still stand. Robert was, as one obituary put it in 1907, a 'pioneer of industry'; 'a man of fine presence and physique', said another, 'of considerable business acumen and tireless industry'. Factories made Keighley, as the stone buildings in the middle of town testify to this day, and the self-made factory owners such as Robert made money. He married a Keighley woman and had three daughters, then three sons. Like other amateur captains of his time, Walter Robins and Norman Yardley, Brian Sellers' family could afford to send him to fee-paying schools and let him play cricket full-time for expenses only. Yet commoners were not far down their family trees. According to the 1871 census, when Arthur was ten months, also in the Sellers household was Arthur's grandmother Mary, 'formerly a laundress'.

The famous Thomas Mann novel Buddenbrooks tells of three generations of a family; the energetic grandfather builds a business, the uninspired son merely manages it, and it falls when the grandson ignores it for the sake of art. The Sellers family was not like that. Everyone from Robert on threw themselves into civic life. Robert was a founder of Keighley's chamber of commerce and a stalwart of the Liberal Club; besides cricket, Arthur was a committee member of Keighley Golf Club; a cousin of Brian's founded a gliding club. Brian's mother Mary – who coached him in the back garden, as his father was so often away playing cricket - was an 'indefatigable charity and church worker'. All this took money. The golf club, that Brian was also a member of, in the 1920s cost three guineas to join besides the six guineas a year subscription; a month's pay for some.

Brian Sellers' surviving son Andrew did not know how much advice Brian got from Arthur. From Brian Sellers' reported after-dinner speeches – one more thing he followed his father in - we can tell that in at least some ways Brian took after his father. 'Don't pack a game in if you are getting old,' Brian Sellers told an annual cricketing dinner in Bradford in September 1958. 'The league and your own clubs have to be run. They have given you a lot of enjoyment so why not put something back into the game?' Sellers offered also some of his philosophy, perhaps the nearest he went that night to a comment on the recent controversial sacking of Johnny Wardle. Enjoy whatever you do, he urged; and, surely, any differences can be sorted out: 'That is the way I was brought up in this game. If you have got any grievance, get it off your chest and bear no malice.'

North Street, Keighley, one of the main streets in the town in the 1900s. Sellers' childhood home was out of town on the left.

In the centre of the picture is the Devonshire Hotel, where Arthur Sellers was elected a member of Keighley cricket club in 1887.

Likewise, some of Arthur Sellers' reported words sounded like his son's. Both men championed good fielding. 'When I was a young player I practised every night I possibly could and we had not the advantages you have nowadays of daylight saving,' Arthur told a prize-giving at Ingrow outside Keighley in 1937: 'A man who made 50 runs by batting and lost 60 on the field was not as good as a man who made only 20 but saved 50.' 'Anyone calling himself a cricketer ought to be able to field,' Brian told the Bradford League annual dinner in 1956.

Arthur Sellers.

Thanks to Robert, the Sellers family could bring up their children in comfort. Brian was born in March 1907 and had an elder brother, Godfrey. According to the 1911 census, Arthur and Mary Sellers, and their two sons, lived in an eight-roomed house with two servants; Robert in the 1871 and 1891 censuses only had one servant. More subtle was Arthur's name and influence that gave Brian a start, ahead of others – unspoken and unwritten, or taken for granted, as such things usually are. That said, to make his way in cricket he had to work the same as anyone else. 'It's a poor do that a lad like me at 48 can throw a cricket ball further than these youngsters. There is not sufficient practice,' he told that 1956 dinner.

Brian Sellers makes an interesting comparison with Norman Yardley, who captained Yorkshire after Sellers from 1948. The men went to the same school, St Peter's, in York; Yardley was eight years younger. In his 1949 memoir *Cricket Campaigns*, while he was captain of England, Yardley recalled playing for his school's first eleven against 'the Craven Gentlemen', captained by Sellers, 'who scored a century in beautiful style', probably in July 1930. Although Yardley wrote of then envying the older man, Sellers only became a Yorkshire player (and captain) at 25, whereas Yardley was capped by Yorkshire at 22 and was playing for England on tour at 23. Yardley rose early, like Arthur Sellers; and went further. From St Peter's Yardley went to Cambridge University; unlike Sellers. It made Yardley one of the few Yorkshiremen who could stand their own, socially and in cricket terms, with Sellers, and it showed in his memoir. Yardley

*North Street, where Brian Sellers grew up.
The villa has recently been a retirement home and by 2015 was empty.*

joked how Sellers was known as Midge while a boy at St Peter's, 'but talking expanded him, and he grew to six feet'. Few men were so merry in print about Sellers. While Sellers, then, did not have quite the elite finishing of Yardley, he had more spent on him than others in his wider family. Herbert Sellers – the cousin who founded the gliding club, who died at 29 in 1933 – went to the boys' grammar school in Keighley. Arthur Sellers sent his son to boarding school, whether out of ambition, or because it simply suited the father to have the boy off his hands most of the time. Likewise, thanks to the war, then going to prep and public school, and service in the Army, Andrew Sellers only started to get to know his father after the age of 20. His brother David was a cricketer – 'I think he played for the Yorkshire colts once or twice' – but Andrew was never really interested, 'mainly I think because he wasn't there to bowl a ball on the lawn or things like that. It never entered my life.'

In the seven seasons from 1925, when Brian Sellers began playing for Keighley's first team, until 1932, when Yorkshire called, he became steadily more successful without standing out as his father did. Looking back, we can see that playing for Keighley – usually on a Saturday and bank holidays, in the Bradford League – did prepare Sellers for his later years. For example, crowds were sometimes of county size, and certainly large by later standards. In June 1925, aged 18, Sellers was batting at five in front of 3000 spectators. A month later, when visitors Queensbury made 230 for seven, Keighley with two hours to bat seemed to have little chance when they were 36 for three after half an hour. 'It was left to two younger members of the side,' Sellers and Allan Shackleton (who played twice for Yorkshire under Sellers nine years later), 'to pull the game around.' Sellers was out at 136 - caught one-handed at third slip – 'for a very fine 45' in 50 minutes.

Sellers was promising enough to be one of 14 amateurs invited to the 'winter shed' at Headingley in April 1926, where the former Yorkshire and England all-rounder George Hirst ran his eye over talented lads. Having averaged 13 in 1925 – not bad in a league where teams often made double figures – Sellers had an unsuccessful 1926. He was in and out of the firsts; admittedly perhaps only because he was doing other things, as he did not feature in the second team averages. In any case he did better in 1927. He did little in the first matches, then batting at four made the second top score out of 191 as Keighley easily beat Baildon Green: 'The crowd were treated to a glorious half hour from Sellers .... Sellers made many brilliant strokes including two drives out of the ground and it was unfortunate that with his score at 24 and his form good enough for a hundred he should have ended his career leg before wicket.'

Sellers was already showing his adult style, 'busy', 'lusty', 'bright and free'. In June 1927 his 33 rescued Keighley as they beat the league leaders Idle. He treated spectators 'to a gloriously fine spell of resolute hitting', bringing up 100 'with a great hit over the boundary in front of the pavilion. Next ball however he attempted to repeat the stroke and was bowled.' In the last match of the season Sellers opened the batting.

He developed further in 1928. In a June innings of 33, 'of correct batsmanship', Sellers 'showed an encouraging habit of being able to sort out the right balls for hitting and never resorted to mere 'slogging''. The local press was beginning to report his outstanding catching and fielding. At Bankfoot in July, the home captain and top scorer played a ball towards Sellers at cover, and set off for a run, to avoid having to face the fast bowler any more: 'Everybody knows of the agility of Sellers and the next moment Smith was walking a sadder and probably wiser man back to the pavilion.' Keighley won narrowly; Sellers was seeing for himself how fielding could turn a match. Besides learning the skills of the game, he was taking in its more subtle culture. In August for example he was out for seven after hitting 'a prodigious drive' into the football field, because he was forcing runs on the brink of victory in case rain came. He was showing himself ready to lose his wicket for the sake of the team. He was learning the rules, sometimes the hard way. In 1929 he was out in an unusual way, when 'he noticed that a bail was not properly in its groove. He put it into its correct position whereupon the wicket-keeper appealed with the result that the square leg umpire gave him out.'

By 1929 Sellers was usually opening the batting. We have a glimpse of his life outside cricket in July when he was once late half an hour on the field, as he had a motor accident on his way to Keighley's Lawkholme Lane ground. Only the well-off could afford to drive then. He was growing in stature, and making bigger scores, as a hard hitter. In August at Bradford Park Avenue 'Sellers surprised the natives by rattling up a half century in three-quarters of an hour – it was one of his best efforts for the club – and he had a great reception when he retired caught on the boundary edge for 57 ...' At home to Bingley in the last match of 1929, he made 'a brilliant 52 in characteristic fashion' out of 148 for six. Keighley finished sixth out of 20 in the league, compared with fifth the season before; Sellers came second in the club's batting averages with 564 runs at 31.33, far better than his 13.32 the year before.

At their most extreme, matches approached the county game in length; in the first round of the Priestley Cup knock-out, over two days at Saltaire in June 1930, Keighley were in the field for 115 overs as Saltaire made 488. Sellers as the seventh bowler took two for 15 in three overs. Sellers then made 16 of Keighley's 403 in 154 overs. He was still fielding tirelessly ('a shining example to his colleagues') and playing the Yorkshire way. For instance, in May he was not out 47 and Keighley 87 without loss when rain stopped play for the day, only when it became 'too heavy'. He was among men who wanted to play; and win; and not lose. In June, after Keighley declared at 201 for eight, the visitors Pudsey St Lawrence batted out the last 14 overs as maidens to draw on 98 for nine. Those watching 'verbally demonstrated their disbelief'.

By 1931 he was captain. Yorkshire invited him to the April nets at Headingley; George Macaulay as part of his benefit was bringing a Yorkshire team to Keighley to play a team that Sellers chose. Sellers was becoming known around the county; only, on the evidence, he did not make runs often enough to demand a place among the first eleven. At Lawkholme he made a 'masterly' 76 in two hours – caught on the boundary from a straight drive after he hit a six over the stand – and 'indulged in a daring experiment' that worked, putting himself on as a bowler to bowl the last man, and so win nine minutes from time; however this 'showed', as the *Keighley News* reported, 'that his discouraging Whitsuntide experience with the county colts had not affected him'. He was out for nought and eight against Lancashire seconds at Redcar, then out for two and one against Nottinghamshire seconds at Rotherham. In July, a week after the *Keighley News* said Sellers was not able to find his true form, he made a 'masterly' 104 against Bradford out of 205, his first century.

That Sellers joined the Yorkshire first team, as captain, had two sides to it: his own claims, and the few other candidates. After the 1914-18 war and before 1932 – that is, 13 seasons – Yorkshire had six captains. Some were figureheads, and everyone knew it. In his 1950 history of Yorkshire between the wars, J.M.Kilburn described the duties on the field of Major A.W.Lupton, the captain from 1925 to 1927, as 'not onerous'. Afterwards, as was well aired, the county offered their professional Herbert Sutcliffe the captaincy; which came to nothing, as members insisted on an amateur. In his early days the press only called Sellers 'acting captain' as he was standing in for Frank Greenwood. Under him, Yorkshire were county champions in 1931 for the first time since 1925. The captaincy for 1932

– Yorkshire only gave it one year at a time – was his. Sellers recalled Greenwood in later life: 'He was in the paint business in Huddersfield with his father and was invited to captain the side in 1932; he was a splendid chap. The players loved him – a county hockey player, a good athlete altogether in all senses of the word.' Greenwood's father died; on 22 March Greenwood resigned. Sellers was not the obvious man to take over. Even his local Keighley News reported 'the name of W.E.Harbord of Wetherby is being freely mentioned'. William Harbord had an impeccable background – Eton and Oxford University – and being born in Rutland had not stopped him playing for Yorkshire. For the seconds in 1931 he made more runs in four innings than Sellers made in seven.

Yorkshire 1920s captain Major AW (Arthur) Lupton.

On Tuesday, April 5, 1932, the Yorkshire cricket committee meeting in Leeds made Brian Sellers vice-captain, which meant he would skipper when Greenwood could not. In a rare interview for the *Yorkshire Post* in 1969 Sellers recalled: 'I didn't bother to ask how I came to be captain.' He only needed to ask his father, the committee chairman.

Sellers told the *Keighley News*: 'It has always been my ambition to play for Yorkshire. I am very glad to be able to follow in my father's footsteps and I only hope I shall do as well as he has done.' It was telling that he never spoke of an ambition to *captain* Yorkshire. As newspapers do, it set out the reasons Sellers gained the job: he was tall and 'of good physique';

he had captained his school eleven aged 16; he was a magnificent cover point fielder, and he had often 'delighted crowds by his free, polished and vigorous batting'. In truth he was untried, and had not earned a place in the Yorkshire first team.

The county was taking less of a risk than it looked. As the *Keighley News* reported, Greenwood would be captain 'for a good many matches'. Sellers could be one more stopgap for a season or two, until he tired of being a captain in name only, someone more qualified came along, or like Greenwood he had to put business first. On that score the press reported only that Sellers was a 'member of the office staff at the Hayfield Mills of JC Horsfall and Sons, Glusburn', makers of wool yarn outside Keighley.

In later life Sellers recalled the details. 'I had a severe entrée to first-class cricket':

My sister-in-law was living above Glasgow. Before we went up there for Easter, which was early, we went to see sister-in-law's parents in Scarborough. I felt not at all well – I felt bloody awful and I went to lay on my sister-in-law's father's bed. We decided we had better get home, I sent for a doctor and he said I had jaundice and to stay where I was. Dad came to see me on the Monday or Tuesday and he was smiling and I thought, 'what's he bloody well got to smile about with me laying on this bed'. He said: 'I've got news for you – the committee in their wisdom or otherwise have appointed you vice-captain.'

'Never.'

'That's the decision. I know you're not good enough, you're not up to standard, but that's their decision.'

I went on up to convalesce in Scotland and came back to practice.

Even if Brian Sellers was putting his father's or his own thoughts into his father's mouth, this was not false modesty. He was not the only man in cricket, let alone anywhere else, who got where he was thanks to who he was, rather than what he did. Robert Scott, the Sussex captain Sellers faced in 1933, was the son of a Sussex vice-president. Sellers was realistic enough to feel unease at the task ahead. As Sellers told the *Yorkshire Post* in 1969: 'Let's face it, there were eight internationals in the side and the others were players of experience. I came along as skipper and rookie. It wasn't the best way to start but it gave me the incentive to get up to their standard as quickly as possible.'

An example of his unease at this time was his dilemma over his county cap. Vividly, though less suitably for print, in old age Sellers recalled his dealings with the secretary Jack Nash ('bless him') and his father. First Nash told Sellers: 'Your father has instructed me to give you your cap':

I said I shan't accept it, take it back, I've got to earn it. And he said, that's what your father has instructed me to do and he'll be angry if I don't, and I told him, it's me that'll get the bollocking when I get home! And by God I did. Dad told me, when I give instructions on behalf of the committee

I expect them to be obeyed. I know you're not good enough but we can't have a captain of Yorkshire going into the field not wearing the county's cap. I don't like it, I said. 'You've no choice,' he said. 'Tomorrow you will go back and apologise to the secretary and accept the cap.' You see it was the principle that mattered.

A club could hardly send its captain onto the field, for all to see, without a club cap, and of lesser status than some of his men. It did Sellers credit that he did not feel equal to the men under him, and understood that capped players might hold his unearned cap against him; but that would not help him much in trying to win their respect. It helped that he looked the part at first sight. When Sellers took Yorkshire to Worcester in 1933, the county's first visit since 1929, *Berrow's Worcester Journal* called Sellers 'a veritable giant'. In Sellers' time, only Bill Bowes at six foot four was a couple of inches taller. Presumably because Yorkshire drew its professionals from the working class, who had hard lives and ate poorly, most were small; of 27 players listed at pre-season practice in 1926, the tallest was five foot 11. Sellers meant business; in a 1931 Keighley team photograph, he kneeled in the centre of five players, his sleeves rolled to the elbows, while most of his men were wearing sweaters. He had physical presence; he had to back it with words and deeds.

Chapter Three
The line that disciplines the fell

Clearly, there is more to being a captain than having an asterisk by your name in the scorebook.
Ray Illingworth, Captaincy (1980)

In Sellers' eight seasons as captain before the 1939-45 war, Yorkshire played 236 Championship matches, winning 137 and losing 21. Few teams in any sport win more than six times as often as they lose, for long. The premier journalist following them, Jim Kilburn of the *Yorkshire Post*, in a 1950 book claimed such success was easy to explain: 'It lay in brilliant fielding, the remarkable form of Herbert Sutcliffe, and the complete development of Bowes and Verity.' Sellers could only claim a part in the fielding.

Was it luck? Yardley in his memoir told a story of how a 'lady admirer' sent Sellers a lucky horseshoe, and then Sellers lost the toss 13 times on the trot; and the team 'quietly abstracted the little token and threw it in the Ouse'. If Sellers had luck, it was that his chance came at the right time; if he had been a few years younger, other amateurs, Yardley (a more able batsman) and Paul Gibb (as wicket-keeper-batsman), would have had better claims to the captaincy. A team of lesser characters might have crumpled, faced by Sellers. Everything came right together.

Just as the largest armies ought to win all the wars, so Yorkshire as a large county with many cricket clubs, and money from regular Test matches, ought always to do well in county cricket. While picking strongest teams may be a way we fill time in a pub on a dark night, or old players fill pages in their memoirs, arguably the strongest county eleven of all time was Yorkshire's against Middlesex in the end of season challenge match at The Oval in September 1937. In batting order: Len Hutton, Herbert Sutcliffe, Arthur Mitchell, Maurice Leyland, Wilf Barber, Norman Yardley, Brian Sellers, Frank Smailes, Arthur Wood, Hedley Verity and Bill Bowes. Only Sellers never played for England. Yardley, Smailes and Wood had yet to play for England; that they stood so far down the order was a sign of strength. Yardley 'looked to me an Englander the first time I saw him', the monocle-wearing C.B.Fry told *London Evening Standard* readers; E.W.Swanton said that Smailes was good enough to bat at four for a lesser side. The month before Swanton praised Wood as a 'thoroughly good batsman': 'He usually reserves his exceptions for the times when Yorkshire are relatively in distress and that is the only reason his average is not higher. If he went in at number five for Leicestershire he would score 1500 runs a season.' They, and Sellers, had licence to score freely after the earlier batsmen had set up the innings. In this, as in other ways, Sellers' Yorkshire resembled the outstanding Australian team of around 2000.

In each case, some – such as the then *London Evening News* journalist E.M.Wellings – reckoned that the side captained itself. It sounded plausible, and appealed to the vanity of the other ten. The more informed Johnny Wardle in his 1957 memoir called that ignorant, 'because there is no side so good that it is not the better for having a great captain'. Jim Kilburn agreed that Sellers inherited success, 'and by doing nothing he could scarcely have failed to acquire a Championship or two; he did much more than that'.

Sellers mattered for several reasons. The very excellence of Yorkshire's players meant that England called on them more. Discounting the washed-out Manchester Test of 1938 (the rain ruined Yorkshire's home match anyway) and the single Test against All-India in 1932 (when Yorkshire gave three players, Kent and Surrey two each, and other counties one), in the 26 home Test matches between 1933 and 1939, Yorkshire filled 71 player places. Next came Gloucestershire with 38 (mostly Walter Hammond), Middlesex with 36, Kent 29 (mostly Les Ames) and Lancashire 18. Yorkshire most obviously lost more players than other counties in 1934, an unusually full summer of five Tests against Australia, by filling 17 places; next came Worcestershire, Kent and Middlesex with six each. Lancashire, the 1934 champions, only filled two places. Yorkshire came fifth, their least successful pre-war season under Sellers. Derbyshire, champions in 1936, seldom lost their best men, filling only ten places over the period. Apart from Yorkshire, only Gloucestershire could ever feel deprived; once, in 1937, when they filled eight places in three Tests, and came fourth in the Championship.

Other handicaps were common to all. Playing typically two three-day matches a week might mean a long train journey from one ground to the next. In August 1947, for example, Yorkshire left Scarborough on Friday after drawing with Derbyshire and arrived in Worcester in the small hours. When the local daily newspaper said 'the visitors gained a big advantage by winning the toss', it might have meant Yorkshire batted first on a cracked pitch; or, most of the team could put their feet up. Over a season, every team had to do the same, and first-class cricket had always been like that; 'toil', Lord Hawke called it in his 1924 memoir. Yorkshire – like other teams – did not make it easier for themselves by playing extra matches for whoever's benefit year it was. For example, on Tuesday evening, 20 August 1946 – after drawing a crucial match against Middlesex at Bramall Lane, Sheffield – the Yorkshire players drove a good 20 miles to Sprotborough, the Sheffield side of Doncaster, for a Wilf Barber testimonial game.

Sellers and his men understood what a season would take out of them. During their second match of 1937, at Oxford, while the team dined with the university's new Yorkshire Society, Sellers said: 'We have a long way to go but I hope that at the finish we shall not be very far from the top. That of course depends on how the other counties treat us.' To end a summer as champions a team had to win most matches. That would take excellent play; hard to make routine. Throughout the 1930s - and before and after - watchers called for 'brighter cricket'. The Worcester journalist T.B.Duckworth for instance grumbled in May 1936: 'Much of modern cricket is apt to be somewhat stereotyped. Often one match is much like another with nothing to lift it above the common level and soon fades into the forgotten.' He had hit upon the profound dilemma of modern sport: how could players be consistently exciting, to consistently excite spectators, when they were tired and carrying injuries? How could they make the extraordinary out of the ordinary, what they were doing week after week? To return to Sellers' first match at Oxford, Verity only bowled five overs in the first innings because of a cut on the top joint of his bowling finger, 'a trivial affair which should be right in a day or two'. In July 1938, when Middlesex beat Yorkshire inside two days at Lord's, in their second innings Hutton (broken finger) and Gibb (cut and bandaged head) could not bat and the impact of ball on bat jarred Leyland's dislocated thumb so much he had to retire. Again, other teams' bowlers injured their muscles and batsmen broke bones. Yorkshire only had themselves to blame if they fielded so close that the ball hit them. Also in July 1938, Phil King (a Yorkshireman who had qualified for Worcestershire) pulled Bowes, 'striking [Ellis] Robinson at short fine leg a hard blow on the chest which felled him to the ground. He was assisted to his feet and desirous of resuming but A.B.Sellers ordered him to the pavilion and called out the 12th man Johnson. Apparently the damage was not serious for he returned later,' and indeed bowled King. Here Yorkshire helped themselves by hiring a masseur, Bright Heyhirst, the Leeds rugby league club trainer. Kilburn credited Sellers with having the committee pay for 'that invaluable extra man carried by Yorkshire', as Bowes called him in a 1950 book. At Bradford in July 1937 Yorkshire had to carry Robinson off the field in agony when he stopped a Laurie Fishlock drive; after half an hour of what the *Sheffield Telegraph* called 'Heyhirst's prompt and expert attention', Robinson was back on the field (and took six wickets and made Surrey follow on). Men shrugged off much else. In June 1934 at Sheffield, when Sussex won by an innings - Yorkshire were without Bowes, Leyland, Sutcliffe and Verity, who were beating Australia at Lord's - Sellers was hit on the finger, 'which has now been sore for a fortnight through continued knocks', the *Sheffield Telegraph* reported. One of Sellers' jobs as captain - besides setting a good example - was to keep everyone going. Sellers' strength of coaxing wins out of players also hid a weakness, that Brian Close shared 30 years later; each man preferred the player with experience, rather than having to take time and trouble over a newcomer. That would explain why Joseph Johnson, a slow-left arm bowler, only ever bowled a dozen overs when he played three times in the later 1930s when Verity was away. At Nottingham in August 1938 while Verity was playing in the timeless Test, Johnson did not bowl at all; yet Nottinghamshire batted for 151.1 overs.

The players could look forward to something; the Sabbath. In old age Sellers reflected:

There is no Sunday rest - no golf, no relaxation, no friendships with other players or other counties. It is so frantic, you see. In 1930 Notts looked certain champs and then there was that car crash involving I think Larwood, Bill Voce and Wheat. Yorkshire banned motor cars below Birmingham – the southern tour excepted as it was so hard to get there by train – such long, weary train journeys then, we'd get into the next port of call two or three in the bloody morning and you'd lose the toss and go straight into the field after you'd had a day in the field the day before. They'd know – it was part of the game – we all did it to each other. But oh – those glorious Sundays ...

It was the highlight that after an evening meal you went for a pint with the opposition, you developed friendships, you listened.

As in other occupations whose workers gather in the pub after a shift, you did not stop working. As Sellers hinted, cricketers were picking up what rivals had to say, and rubbing in any advantage. Yardley recalled after the first day of the crucial August 1946 draw against Middlesex, Sellers and Arthur Booth put on 60 for the ninth wicket, that proved enough to give Yorkshire the first innings points. Walter Robins the Middlesex captain was furious:

That evening, Sellers offered Robins a drink. He said he would have a gin, to which Sellers instantly responded, 'Booth's, presumably?' Brian Sellers is one of the quickest-witted cricketers I have ever met, and Yorkshire is the right place for such a man; his quips were gathered after every match and sent flying all round the County, to the accompaniment of laughter and much banging of pint pots.

Yorkshire past and present players at their annual golf day, at Ilkley, Tuesday 3 October 1933. At the back, Scorer Ringrose, George Hirst, Arthur Dolphin, unknowns, Brian Sellers, Emmett Robinson, unknowns – presumably golfers? The ever-dapper Herbert Sutcliffe stands to the left of the cup. At the front are David Denton, Wilf Barber, Arthur Wood, Maurice Leyland, Percy Holmes and Frank Dennis.

Sellers' son Andrew recalled his father as a good and keen golfer: 'Taught me a lot of ways of how to play golf without cheating [chuckles].' In March 1947, Sellers returned from Australia, where he had covered the MCC tour for a Yorkshire newspaper, with a new set of golf clubs. In July 1932 the *Nottingham Evening News* picked up that Sellers was among Yorkshire players on the Rushcliffe links from 10am until late on the Sunday. Sellers had a handicap of one:

He possesses exactly the right physique for the game being tall and lithe. He hits a tremendously long ball from the tee and is exceptionally good through the greens. Yesterday he drove the second and 16th greens which measure 230 yards and 338 yards respectively.

By 1938, Sellers' handicap was two, still far lower than most of the Yorkshire cricketers who played an annual autumn match against golf professionals of the county. The lifelong cricket man, Sir Henry Leveson-Gower, gave a cup that amateur golfers played for on the Sunday of the Scarborough Festival at nearby Ganton golf club. In his memoir, *On and Off the Field*, Sir Henry thanked Sellers for getting up teams: 'It isn't a very easy job for him but it has made all the difference, for very many people come and play for him.'

Who would not want an invitation from Sellers, the man of success, who liked to talk over a pint? In sport, as in politics and in life, many want to pretend in public that everyone in their team, or party, or country, is happy and of one mind. To his credit Sellers was more honest ('get it off your chest and bear no malice'). Eleven or more men, in each other's company only because they came from the same county and were good at the same thing, were never going to see eye to eye always; and even if they did, they might grow sick of the same faces. From looking at five of Sellers' team – a mix of old and young, batsmen and bowlers, senior and junior – we can go deeper than the surface jollity of golf and beery banter, and seek truths about Sellers' leadership.

Herbert Sutcliffe

In later life, Sellers remembered Sutcliffe's nickname, revealingly, was 'The Mayor':

.... he was the greatest Yorkshire batsman of my time and he was Herbert Sutcliffe; but even he would come in and analyse his failure. I remember Maurice Leyland's benefit against Notts, Larwood bowled The Mayor with a straight full-toss that sent his wickets cart-wheeling. 'Oh Christ,' I thought, 'we're for it now,' as Herbert came in. But Herbert said: 'I can't understand it – I should never have got out – if ever there was a six on the cord! Why I missed it I shall never know.' You see Herbert was very critical of his own performance.

That story – from Saturday, June 30, 1934, at Headingley – neatly sums up Sutcliffe and his place in the Yorkshire dressing room. *He was Herbert Sutcliffe*; Sellers did not need to spell out his feats as England opener with

Herbert Sutcliffe.

Jack Hobbs. In June 1932 at Bristol, when Sutcliffe went for a run that wasn't there, and ended up beside his fellow opener Wilf Barber, the other man stepped out of his crease, to give up his wicket for the senior man. And yet Sutcliffe was a batsman like any other. 'Sleek Herbert' C.B.Fry called him; 'imperturbably imperial' according to Howard Marshall in the *Daily Telegraph* in 1937; 'not so sprightly as in days gone by' said the *Northampton Chronicle and Echo* in 1939, even as the 44-year-old made a century. Like others, Arthur Mailey the Australian spinner saw a contradiction in 'Herby' Sutcliffe; he 'was never a pro at heart, although his style of batting suggested it'. Off the field, too, he appeared of a high rank; mayoral. He attended winter cricket dinners like Sellers and other players; only he was invited to speak at an Oxford luncheon club.

Given this man looked and acted like a captain, but was not captain, we might expect that Sutcliffe did not get on with Sellers. Many have repeated the story of how Sutcliffe as the senior professional, that the others looked to, made everyone wait while Sellers stood embarrassingly alone in the middle at Lord's, because Sellers did not see his men in their (separate) dressing room before taking the field. That was not so much a defiance of Sellers as an insisting that everyone – including the captain – knew their place. When Sutcliffe died, Sellers paid tribute to the 'great help' Sutcliffe gave him as captain. Sutcliffe in his 1935 autobiography, *For England and Yorkshire*, seemingly wrote well enough of Sellers 'as one of the best fieldsmen in the game, and, in addition, he is a batsman of ability as he showed in the game with the Australians at Sheffield last season, for then he scored a fighting century when runs were needed.' What Sutcliffe did not say – anything about Sellers as captain – was as significant; as was his judgement that a young captain 'must be prepared when he enters county cricket to spend five years in learning his job'. By that reckoning, Sellers was then still a learner. Sutcliffe also talked up A.T.Barber, who captained Yorkshire to third in 1930, as a 'first-class' and 'great' captain. Was that Sutcliffe's way of putting Sellers in his place?

In later life Sellers did admit to one clash, on a big subject; money.

The thing had always been that all the first team were on the same pay – Herbert Sutcliffe and Cyril Turner [a useful but far from regularly playing all-rounder] *got the same and Herbert never disagreed with this for instance. The committee used to offer £200 a season to me to distribute as talent money - £200 among say 14 players .... this was the only occasion that Herbert was not very pleased – he would get about £15.*

In other words, Sutcliffe felt he didn't get his due. Did he feel he should have been captain? According to Leslie Duckworth, who met Sutcliffe in the late 1960s for his book *The Run Stealers*, Sutcliffe wished he had stuck to his original acceptance of Yorkshire's offer in 1927. After Sellers, Sutcliffe was next in line. In July 1935, Sutcliffe was captain at Nottingham when Sellers damaged an ankle and did not play. After Larwood hit Mitchell on the back of the hand so that he could not field, Sellers fielded as substitute, under Sutcliffe.

An intriguing story made the front page of the *London Evening News* on Friday 11 August 1939. Sutcliffe, injured and at home, gave a short interview. That newspaper – and many others that picked up the story – speculated that, like Hammond, Sutcliffe might turn amateur (although Sutcliffe called that 'Tommy rot') and then become captain. Yorkshire that day were playing at Leicester. The local *Leicester Mercury* put it to Sellers: was he retiring, to make way for Sutcliffe? 'It is entirely new to me, the first I have heard of it,' Sellers replied. Sutcliffe likewise denied it, as unfair to Sellers, while admitting 'at various times in recent years' he had thought of turning amateur; but not since August 1938.

What can we make of this? Had the original reporter made a meal of at best a year-old story? Was Sutcliffe testing opinion? And why then, with war plainly so near? At the least we can say that Sutcliffe felt – or others felt it for him – that he deserved to be of officer rank, as he was in the 1914-18 war. In May 1936, while Yorkshire were in Oxford, a story made the newspapers from the county's recent winter tour of Jamaica. Sutcliffe in disguise had batted in a Sherwood Foresters battalion match between officers, and the warrant officers and sergeants. The *Oxford Mail* reported how the publicity amused Sutcliffe. He did correct one detail; 'actually I turned out for the officers'.

Bill Bowes

In 1934 the Nottinghamshire captain Arthur Carr rated Bowes as 'our', meaning England's, 'best new ball bowler'. Carr described him as 'fast medium' rather than fast, who could however thanks to his height bowl a 'nasty length'. Spectators around the country for years jeered Bowes for bowling short and nearly or actually hitting the batsman. E.W.Swanton reported a most blatant example, at The Oval in August 1932:

Bowes who had not seemed likely to get a wicket by ordinary methods began to bowl wicked-looking bouncers which pitched well short of halfway. The spectators showed their displeasure at these methods in no half-hearted manner ... Hobbs treated the short ones with amused contempt and twice after successive balls had whistled over his head he walked slowly up the wicket and deliberately patted the ground on the good length spot the other end. To the third ball Hobbs had to duck in a great hurry and then seemed to have a few words with Bowes, probably a reminder that they were engaged on a game of cricket and not a baseball match.

Was Bowes trialling Bodyline in front of Douglas Jardine? Either way, Sellers must have approved. Sometimes he made Bowes bowl long spells; an hour and a quarter in that case against Surrey. Two games later at Hove, Sellers gave Bowes an hour and a half on the second evening, and another

Douglas Jardine.

hour and a quarter the next morning. Sellers made Bowes work because he could take it, in this case bowling 'with undiminished fire and pace in broiling hot sunshine'. Sellers also did it because so often it worked; Bowes took early wickets, of the best batsmen, before spinners went to work on the rest.

Sellers might ask less of lesser bowlers. Without Bowes at Sheffield in June 1932, in his place Charles Hall took six for 71; who 'owed a good deal of his effectiveness ... to the careful way in which Sellers nursed him', the *Sheffield Telegraph* reported.

For most of the 1930s, Bowes was not a Yorkshire player, but a member of the MCC staff, as Lord's signed him – on an extraordinarily long, nine-year contract. As Bowes and Verity were the only bowlers to feature among the leading three wicket-takers for Yorkshire every season from 1932 to 1939, Yorkshire did not seem that clever at spotting talent.

What did Bowes make of it all – not being spotted at first, the hard work that always risked injury, the hoots from the crowd? At Hove in 1935, when he hit the Sussex captain A.J.Holmes (already injured) under the chin, the *Sussex Daily News* reporter approached Bowes in the pavilion afterwards; 'he politely indicated that he had nothing to say'. For this sandy-haired man in spectacles who later became a journalist, not being allowed an opinion might have felt like one more injustice. Bowes could brood – 'the Knight of the Mournful Countenance', C.L.R.James once called him – but you might brood, if you had kept a diary on the Bodyline tour that a thoughtless teammate lost out of the window as the train home went through the Rockies.

As for many men, even if the 1939-45 did not change him, life around him changed for him. Reviewing near the season's end in August 1946, Kilburn called Bowes 'a source of great comfort to his captain'. In August 1947 at Worcester, the local evening 'paper took Yorkshire's picture before they took the field. Bowes was Sellers' right-hand man. As so often in life, the measure of this man was how others missed him when he was gone.

Hedley Verity

Although a left-arm spin bowler, Verity had much in common with Bowes. Neither man came from quite a working-class or middle-class home: Bowes was the son of a goods foreman at a Leeds railway depot; Verity's father was a Leeds coal merchant. Jardine praised Verity as observant. Few batsmen could do more than defend against him, and Sellers used that as long and often as he used Bowes. Worcestershire in June 1937 was typical; after Yorkshire made 460, Verity came on and whipped a ball across Eddie

Cooper's stumps: 'Sellars [sic] immediately crowded in the fielders around the batsman and in the same over Cooper jumped out desperately and was bowled,' off the fourth ball of Verity's fourth over, before he had given away a run. He took ten wickets in the match as Yorkshire won by an innings.

Verity, then, was a bowler of power. Did Sellers, understandably, ask too much of him, as 'his stock bowler', as Sir Home Gordon claimed in *The Cricketer* magazine in May 1937? By August 1939 E.M.Wellings claimed to see 'a sign of staleness' in Verity.

Charles Barnett, Gloucestershire and England batsman.

Verity was good-natured, men agreed. In his 1936 book *Bowling 'Em Out*, he must have been writing of himself as 'the chap who just smiles and keeps on doing his best', despite dropped catches. Like Sutcliffe, however, Verity wrote suspiciously little about Sellers. Was that only out of caution, so as not to make trouble; because he had little good to say; or as a deliberate snub? An admiring 1952 biography of Verity ended with tributes from his old headmaster, his father, Yorkshire president Sir Stanley Jackson, fellow England players Sutcliffe and Charles Barnett, and his regiment; not Sellers, whose tribute *Wisden* (no less) had printed. Was Sellers not welcome? In January 1947, while Sellers was reporting in Australia on the MCC tour, the occasional bowler Norman Yardley sensationally got Bradman out twice. Sellers wrote that everyone was asking if Yardley would open the bowling for Yorkshire the next season (actually, Yardley had a few times already):

I have had to remind them with a smile that Hedley Verity opened the England innings out here on one tour and that when he returned to Yorkshire I said to him that he might be number one for England but he was still number ten for Yorkshire!

Even the best-natured man might close his heart to someone who could sound so unfeeling.

Len Hutton

Bowes and Verity had made their names before Sellers arrived; Hutton made his under Sellers. Hutton however looked to Sutcliffe. 'Little Herbert', C.B.Fry called Hutton in August 1936. In his second match, at Oxford in May 1934, the *Oxford Mail* reported how 'Yorkshire have the greatest faith in him as a number one batsman of the near future'. Four years later, the same newspaper praised him as 'an England number one all right'.

His rise in between was not quite as smooth as it looked afterwards. On his Championship debut at Edgbaston in May 1934, batting at five, he made 50; however the *Birmingham Post* complained of Yorkshire's slow scoring. Worst of all, 'at the height of the afternoon when there were only five wickets down and over 300 runs on the board the champion county of England was represented by a partnership that scored eight runs in 25 minutes!'. That was between Hutton and Sellers, who was caught for three off George Paine – another example of him falling to a slow bowler.

Len Hutton and Alderman Myers, Mayor of Pudsey, at the dinner in honour of Hutton in October 1938.

Hutton was not quite 18. The county evidently saw his talents – his temperament as much as his sound batting – and gave him time to blossom, so that by the 1937 challenge match, when he anchored the innings with 121, the *Daily Worker* could praise him as 'very good indeed. He has modelled his defensive strokes on Sutcliffe's and has a lovely drive through the covers that travels very fast and that he seems in no danger of mistiming.' At the timeless Test against Australia in August 1938, Hutton made his monumental, Bradman-beating 364. His hometown of Pudsey put on a dinner for him; Sellers was among the speakers. According to the *Yorkshire Post*, Sellers gave the 22-year-old some 'sound advice': 'Don't live in the past. Forget what you have done and the records you have made and broken. Get stuck into what is before you.' Sellers was the mouthpiece for the Yorkshire way of cricket; never satisfied, always looking for the next triumph. For one night, among Hutton's kith and kin, could Sellers not have given it a rest?

English and Australian cricketers alike observed that Hutton's upbringing in 'the hard Yorkshire school' moulded the man as the first professional captain of England, though not his county. As Trevor Bailey put it, Hutton learned to give 'nowt' and to expect 'nowt'. As important as how his team treated others was how the team got on among itself. Hutton in old age recalled how the captain as an amateur dressed in a different room. Hutton believed this physical distance helped, as it gave the professionals freedom to talk: '... if the captain had been present, those views would have been bottled up or, if aired, provoked bad feeling'. That implied players sometimes spoke ill of Sellers, even if only in the heat of a moment. Hutton did recall good advice from him. On 25 July 1934 at Worcester, Hutton needed a morale-boosting innings after an unsuccessful month as opener: 'Sellers told me to go in and play my own game.' Hutton made 196, his highest score of his first three seasons.

Sellers, then, mattered to all four of these men, although as players they each achieved more than him. The four had one thing in common that they did not share with Sellers. They were Freemasons.

Freemasonry

Bradman, Hammond, Ranji and Colin Cowdrey, to name only a few famous cricketers, were Freemasons. Of all the words written about them, you would expect something about that fact, even if membership were unimportant to them. Ignorance is no longer any excuse, as it's been no secret since 2012, when the Library and Museum of Freemasonry put online a list of hundreds of famous sporting Freemasons.

We can only speculate beyond the bare details: Bowes joined a West Riding lodge in 1935; Verity, the same lodge in 1939. Hutton joined a Pudsey lodge in 1942. Sutcliffe joined a London lodge and indeed became lodge master. Bryan Stott, a Yorkshire batsman and long-time Freemason of a later generation, confirmed those names in 2016 and added two: Cyril Turner and Frank Smailes. Was Sutcliffe, the older man, the influence on others? Or was membership of another all-male secretive group – an MCC touring party – the cause? Two 1930s captains in Australia and former Oxbridge men, Jardine and Gubby Allen, were Freemasons. Even if you find Freemasonry unimportant and silly, it's worth studying like any group, that included some, and excluded others. At least one of Sellers' family was a Freemason: his uncle Herbert, his father's older brother, according to his 1930 obituary, was a member of a lodge in Keighley. We cannot say how widespread Freemasonry was among Yorkshire or any other cricket people, or if it mattered; and not for any sinister reason, but because we can never be sure we know everything. The Earl of Harewood, a patron of the county club, was a provincial grand master, although he was a figurehead for many other bodies.

Sellers was not a Freemason, nor his father, nor indeed Yorkshire's next captain Norman Yardley; or to be exact, the Library of Freemasonry in London reports that their names do not feature in indexes of members.

Were Sellers, father and son, not Freemasons because they felt it was not for them; or because members did not want them? We cannot know if Freemasonry was a bond between Bowes, Verity, Sutcliffe or Hutton; or even if they knew each was a member. Whether they joined because they believed in it; because they wanted to rise in society generally; or they liked the company, of clubbable conservative men that made a change from cricketers: they made themselves a life that did not belong to Yorkshire cricket club; or Brian Sellers.

Ellis Robinson

Whenever he was in a Yorkshire team photograph, Ellis Robinson was usually smiling broadly, as if he were glad to be there. He was a worthy member, as a hard-hitting lower order bat, an outstanding catcher, and above all as an off-spinner. In the three seasons from 1937 until the war, he was one of the four men who bowled most balls for the county; in Sellers' last two seasons after the war, Robinson took most wickets. Even then, Robinson sometimes suffered according to the order of seniority. In the list in the newspapers of the 13 for that 1937 challenge match, the amateurs Sellers and Yardley came first, then the most senior professionals – first Sutcliffe, then Leyland and Wood – to the last two, Cyril Turner and Robinson, who were indeed the two left out of the eleven. The twelfth man had the traditional and thankless job of looking after the bags on the journey to the next match; and had to ask the players for the money afterwards, for any taxis or porters. 'The established people, they didn't have to do it. You wouldn't expect Herbert to do it, would you?' Robinson said.

The most a man could do was excel when he did have a chance; even then you might not keep your place. Dickie Bird learned that, a generation later, in May 1959 when he made 181 not out, what proved his highest score for Yorkshire:

When I got back to the dressing room, Brian Sellers, the chairman of selectors, was there to greet me. 'Well played, Dickie lad,' he said. 'But get thee bloody head down, you're in the second eleven in the next match.' That's Yorkshire cricket: they deflate you before you can reflect in any glory. Sellers had a lot of enemies but I liked and respected him. He gave it to you straight, never behind your back. That is another admirable Yorkshire quality.

Robinson put something similar into print: 'I got 13 wickets in one match and at half past six I was told that I wasn't required for the next match, that I was playing in the seconds. You couldn't sort of fathom why; it was probably to stop you getting big headed.' While Bird and Robinson understood why Sellers did it to them well enough, the reasons were fundamentally economic and cultural; Sellers as the foreman for the employer was denying the workers any feeling of security; or rights, of expression for example. Robinson recalled how (in June 1939) Yorkshire lost at Bristol on a pitch made for the off-spinner Tom Goddard (who took 13 wickets); yet they left out Robinson. 'You couldn't say anything. The captain, chairman of selectors, chairman of the committee, was a virtual dictator,' Robinson said in later life. Arlott in old age likewise looked back on 'a strange, feudal world', of 'tyranny' of senior professionals over juniors, and by some amateur captains over all professionals. And yet, as in wider society, at least in such a tyranny, everyone knew their place. Even if the lowest-ranked men felt put upon, at least they could feel they had prospects of rising. For how else do men know that they are of a higher rank, unless they have someone of lower rank to order around – to mind their bags and suitcases? Captains, as E.W.Swanton recalled, could play more subtle parts than mere tyrants; the best 'were very much the guardians of their flocks'. That condescending metaphor – likening the players to sheep – says much about Swanton, and his generation and class. Though seldom spelt out – because that would put workers on a par with the bosses – Swanton, Sellers and his kind were not crediting the likes of Robinson with feelings. The Yorkshire committee man Sid Fielden, who knew Robinson, recalled him saying: 'I wish he [Sellers] would have liked me a bit.' The tragedy is not only that Robinson felt unwanted – although that evidently mattered to Robinson, a man of mood swings, 'either in the clouds or way down in the dumps', as came out in a March 1947 drink-driving court case. It's a reminder that the men under Sellers, as in any sports team or any group, were human; that is to say, imperfect. As it happens, Fielden (who knew Sellers also) thought that Sellers *did* like Robinson. The tragedy lies in Robinson looking to his captain for feelings. Sellers, if he did really like anyone, could not show it, for then he would have favourites. Team equality, for Sellers, meant treating men equally roughly. As Robinson knew from the hurt of being cast out of the first team, even after winning a match for Yorkshire, the team came before any single man; it had to, if Yorkshire were to be better than the rest. Poignantly, Robinson could not help but wish for love.

Eleven outstanding cricketers are not the same as a champion team. The eleven had to agree to set tactics – keeping match-winning always in mind while doing the routines of batting, or bowling and fielding – and strategy, keeping a longer Championship-minded, perspective. Someone also had to set the tempo; to put it another way, Sellers was like the coachman flogging the horses. It's a truth seldom admitted, because who wants to think of themselves as no better than whipped animals? Yet the same is true in politics, and business, perhaps any field of life; to get anything extraordinary done, the one in charge, the one with the ideas, has to bully others – who draw their pay no matter what – into giving more. The very fact that this team did such great things together, awakened a sense that they were special, that could prompt the players to feel warmly towards each other. Ironically, Yorkshire could only win, and keep winning, by shunning such feelings, as sentimental, and unhelpful. Not the least of Sellers' tasks as captain was to tread on anything that might weaken them; to be the line that disciplines the fell. If you defied the skipper or did badly on the field, 'you didn't last very long'; so Robinson recalled. Someone could always take the place of another.

Sellers, appointed one year at a time, had no more job security than anyone else. The captain submitted to the discipline, the same as the least of the eleven. Just as the work of the twelfth man, Robinson or whoever, was never done – bags would not follow their owners by themselves - so Sellers had always to drive his team, to the next win, in the next town.

Chapter Four
On the field

A good side works like a good machine, but this
is not to say that it works mechanically.
Douglas Jardine

'One saw at a glance why Yorkshire could win a Championship and hold it,' the Australian journalist A.G.Moyes wrote after rain saved the tourists at Sheffield in July 1938. 'They looked a team.' As so often, the exceptions gave insights into the rule, and the exceptions were Yorkshire's matches against tourists and at the Scarborough festival. The former England captain Freddie Brown recalled how Sellers enjoyed himself at Scarborough, 'quite often in a funny little red schoolboy's cap'. Once, when Brown was waiting to bat for the Gentlemen versus Players, in September 1938, Sellers

.... was batting with the late Denys Wilcox, who hit a ball to the far corner of the ground with mid-on setting off on a long chase. The sight of Sellers going up and down the wicket with enormous long strides, and of Wilcox doing likewise with short fast ones, was an absolute joy, and what made it even better was that Sellers lapped Wilcox by the time he had completed a third run. On ran Sellers regardless, until Wilcox, so overcome with laughter, could run no more. He was put down in the scorebook as 'run out' ....

Even at Scarborough, Sellers was no less keen to make runs – and to get men out. When Brown was batting for the South against the North, in September 1946, Brown was called for a second run:

The bowler, standing about four yards away from the wicket was about to catch the ball when a shriek from the fielding captain, Sellers, persuaded him to duck and let the return go through. The ball hit the wicket when I was still about a yard out. I've always had a look to see who was at third man ever since.

The South African captain Dudley Nourse called Sellers 'one of the most likeable personalities I have ever met on any tour', 'an able leader' and 'a real humourist', and recalled his sharp single in July 1947 at Bramall Lane:

He fled down the wicket to the delight of the spectators and continued his run on to the soccer pitch which forms part of that huge arena and there played by himself an imaginary game of soccer. It was all done quite spontaneously and we enjoyed the fun quite as much as the crowd did.

The eve of a match, the toss, could be a time for fun with a like-minded fellow captain, such as Surrey's Errol Holmes. In one of his playing days memoirs, Hutton told the harmless story of how, as the two captains walked out to toss, Holmes stopped at the blackboard that told the spectators which side had won, and turned it as if he had won. Sellers turned it the other way. While the toss might matter, as an affair of pure chance anyone could do it; at a benefit match, the beneficiary did. In July 1937 at Bradford Park Avenue, Arthur Mitchell won with Sellers' 'lucky four shilling piece'. Even at this stage of a match, Sellers could try hard, whether to seek advantage or simply wind up the other captain. A coin tossed by Arthur Carr, of Nottinghamshire and England, glanced off a wooden bench:

Obviously I could not control the fall of the coin in any way because this happened and it was the same for both sides. When Sellars [sic] claimed that it was a 'foul' I did not agree but I tossed again and again won the toss. You would not like me to toss again for you, would you, I am afraid I said, somewhat sarcastically.

Andrew Sellers recalled his father 'was good at that, just getting somebody going a bit'. Crying foul at the toss did work sometimes. In 1938 Yorkshire's opening match of the season against MCC at Lord's began 15 minutes late, officially 'due to a disagreement regarding the validity of the first toss won by the MCC. The captains tossed again and Yorkshire won.' Somerset player Frank Lee recalled how Sellers trespassed both physically – entering the home professionals' dressing room at Taunton – and culturally when in July 1946 he told the umpires he wanted to see and select the balls for that game, 'a most unusual practice'. Sellers, missing Bowes, was perhaps trying to overawe the home players, to make up for his weak bowlers. 'The box containing the balls was duly produced,' Lee wrote, "and Sellers instructed the umpires, 'we shall use that one to start with, this ball to follow on and this other one should the need arise.'" Somerset made 508 before rain caused a draw.

On and off the field overlapped, most obviously when the players passed to and from the pavilion to the field. In his 1941 profile of Sellers, Robertson-Glasgow praised Sellers' perfect attitude to the game. He was generous in victory and 'in defeat, which is rare, he is more generous still'. Because any defeat of Yorkshire was news, reporters noted how Yorkshire took it. On 30 August 1946, Yorkshire lost for the first time since 1939, at Bournemouth. Sellers was first to shake the hand of Hampshire's captain, Desmond Eagar, who was batting. You could say that Yorkshire had already won that season's Championship, and could afford to lose. Not so at Lord's in June 1937. Sellers, the not out batsman when Yorkshire lost by an innings, walked over to Middlesex captain Walter Robins and shook hands. Likewise in June 1939 at Bristol when the Gloucestershire crowd slapped Wally Hammond and Jack Crapp on the back after they made the winning runs; the Yorkshire fielders joined in the clapping. To beat Yorkshire was an even bigger deal for an also-ran county like Worcestershire. On a spinner's pitch at Stourbridge, Yorkshire lost by 11 runs in May 1936. Sellers praised the winners' fighting spirit to *Berrow's Worcester Journal*: 'A few years ago, your team would have lost that match easily.' Much the same happened in July 1939. The cheering home crowd in front of the pavilion called first for their own captain, then Sellers, who came out and 'waved cheerily, showing that he could take defeat as well as victory'. Sellers, and his men, would also acknowledge good play by the other side. At Leicester in August 1946 Sellers drove straight and hard, only for Tony Riddington to take a one-handed caught and bowled. Sellers tapped his bat to applaud. He clapped with the crowd, whether for a single good shot, such as an off-drive for four by Maurice Tompkin at Leicester in August 1938, or a century that was holding up the win, such as by the Yorkshireman Norman Kilner for Warwickshire at Edgbaston in June 1933. The most obvious example of how Sellers, his team and the followers of Yorkshire felt alike came at Bramall Lane in August 1946. Sellers had claimed the last half hour only for Middlesex's ninth wicket pair to hold out. At the end the crowd of 5500 cheered and the fielders clapped the unbeaten batsmen to the pavilion. And Sellers appreciated the achievements of rivals. When Yorkshire looked like losing at Lord's in July 1938, Sellers was batting when Jim Smith took his 100th wicket of the season. As the Middlesex fielders crowded around to congratulate, Sellers too gave Smith a handshake.

That did not mean Yorkshire were easy-going. That Stourbridge crowd in 1936 'chipped' Sellers in the field as Worcestershire hit 11 sixes in their first innings of an hour and a half and less than 30 overs. Sellers smiled back and said: 'Aye and we shall have a few.' Sussex's ten wicket win at Hull in June 1933 appeared to end simply – the openers Ted Bowley and John Langridge made 17. In fact, the *Yorkshire Post* reported, the batsmen breathed a sigh of relief, as Macaulay and Verity made them work. Such was 'Yorkshire hardness'. Jim Kilburn, who as he put it in his 1972 book *Thanks to Cricket* 'joined' the Yorkshire team in 1934 'as an observer', took care to define it. If to others the players looked aggressive, they were only playing to the best of their ability. They enjoyed being excellent. Others could not see this. At Cambridge in May 1934, after Cambridge took most of the first day to be all out for 248, Yorkshire made 495 for eight by the end of the second day. The *Cambridge News* reporter saw a 'deadly seriousness' in how Yorkshire played the students:

After tea with the score on 400 they were playing just as if they were starting the innings. Some of the Counties which visit Cambridge finding themselves in the position which Yorkshire occupied in the middle of the afternoon and finding how completely they had 'collared' the Light Blue bowling would have changed their tactics. They would have what is called entered into the spirit of the game and tried to liven things up for the benefit of the crowd. Not so Yorkshire. Their outlook is different and they continued to play 'according to the book'.

Sellers, who ended on 52 not out, was batting at that time. 'Nobody can blame them for this,' the Cambridge reporter added. As it happened, Sellers declared overnight with perfect timing, as Cambridge left Yorkshire 14 to win.

Some did find fault, including the *Cambridge News*, in May 1936. After their first innings, Cambridge could have followed on, early on the third

Brian Sellers.

day; instead Yorkshire batted, slowly, and declared and settled for a draw. The *News* said: 'No, no Yorkshire! That is not what we expect from a county of your standing and it must have been a mistake on the part of Sellers.' The newspaper did not ask Sellers; instead it speculated that Sellers was saving his men after a day in the field, and gave them batting practice before they faced Lancashire at Leeds the next day. Sellers, then, did, and said, everything for a reason.

As late as April 1956, when *The Times* previewed the counties, it wrote of how Surrey was reviving Sellers' approach of the 1930s, 'interested only in final victory'. When fielding, that meant taking wickets. Ray Lindwall quoted Sellers characteristically making his point with humour: 'We always see that anyone taking a benefit match gets one off the mark ... and we often give away singles, so that we can shift a batsman to the end we want him!' Some compared the two. 'How often have Yorkshire been described as the Australians of England?' the *Sheffield Telegraph* asked rhetorically in June 1934, while the Australians were playing in the city.

Sellers made plain that Yorkshire played to win, as he told the dinner for Hutton's 364; and 'if they lost they lost like men'. Like so many remarks, that hinted at two sides; how Sellers defined his masculinity, and how he and Yorkshire came across to others. What Sellers and Robins said to the press before their 1937 challenge match showed Yorkshire hardness and how it contrasted with other, more polite, counties. Robins said that he hoped to win; Sellers simply said: 'Easy, no trouble.' Like so much in this story, the hardness that Sellers stood for stretched into the Victorian past and long after him. Nottinghamshire had not beaten Yorkshire at

Trent Bridge since 1891; apart from their fast bowlers Larwood and Voce, most Nottinghamshire players were 'in the grip of a strange inferiority complex', the *Nottingham Journal* claimed in June 1933.

Sellers must have inherited much of what Yorkshire hardness stood for, or already knew it from Keighley. He took his first Championship in August 1932 by winning 14 of the last 15 matches – and rain ruined the other. Early in that streak, Yorkshire beat Gloucestershire at Bradford. In a 1948 book Wally Hammond – who by then could have held a grudge against Sellers – praised Yorkshire for deserving the victory, 'if ever a team did'. After tea, Sellers was making his fielders run across the pitch to change their places between overs, to save in all a few minutes – and Yorkshire won by 133 runs, with minutes to spare.

You could only win by playing; at Northampton in July 1938 Yorkshire went on fielding until the rain was falling sharply, and returned to the field despite slight rain. That is not to say Yorkshire played no matter what. In June 1937 at Nottingham, the home batsmen came off for bad light for a quarter of an hour in the evening. Spectators complained. When Nottingham papers asked Sellers, presumably hoping he would complain too, he said 'we should have done exactly the same'. As significant as his frankness was a sign of how Yorkshire got on with the job: 'Those of us near the wicket had been unable to see for half an hour before they came off.'

Some pitches crumbled so much that batsmen could not last three days; some were so easy to bat on, a draw was almost certain. A team became champions by forcing wins between the two extremes. It took some doing, bowling sides out twice, and scoring more runs than them, inside about 18 hours of play – less for bad weather. Sometimes, margins would be tight; whoever turned most draws into wins would come first. And here Sellers came in, as 'something of a slave-driver', as Bill Bowes put it in his autobiography, *Express Deliveries*. Sellers made the difference by urging fielders to hurry and bowlers to try harder, when those players might have settled for a near-win. In any workplace carrying on a routine, the temptation is to have as easy a working life as you can get away with; and to seize any chance to rest your legs. The umpires, often old players, were no better; Yorkshire won by an innings at Leicester in August 1938, despite a slight delay on the last day because an overnight storm soaked umpire Len Braund's coat in the dressing room; and play had to wait until it was dry. Contrast that unhurriedness – did Braund have to wear a coat to umpire?! - with Bill Edrich's word-picture inside the pavilion at Bramall Lane - most likely 9 July 1937, a rained-off final day - of 'sheeting rain' stopping play, and Sellers 'prowling restlessly about as he always does when rain wastes cricket time'. Sellers did not only have 16 other counties to beat, but the invisible treacle of plodding life that can surround us all.

Sellers was only passing on the slave-driving from above: from the committee and president. In 1937, Yorkshire became champions again, after coming third to Derbyshire and Middlesex the season before. Lord Hawke, re-elected president for a 41st year, could tell the club's annual

Len Braund and A.E.Street, umpires at Lord's, June 1926.

meeting in January 1938: '... last year I felt obliged to comment on the slow play at times when very often more dash might have won the match. This year therefore I am pleased to say that an improved rate of scoring often enabled a victory to be obtained.'

Sellers made sure that Yorkshire seized a winning position, whoever made it. If Yorkshire batted first, they made runs at their tempo. Reporters called it cautious; painstaking; 'no hurry or worry', according to the *Sussex Daily News*, in August 1935. Yorkshire, already champions, made 220 in 102.1 overs – Mitchell's 75 'occupied three weary hours' – after Sussex made 274 in 95.5. How can we explain such slow batting besides Yorkshire's will to win? First, teams then were bowling overs much faster than since – each of those innings took less than a day, and but for rain someone most likely would have won that match. Batsmen seeking runs too eagerly risked losing their wickets, which would set Yorkshire back the same as too slow batting would. Only the commanding total mattered, that gave Yorkshire time to bowl out the other team twice. At Nottingham in July 1934, for example, Sellers only declared one hour after lunch on the second day, when Yorkshire stood at 384 for six after 166 overs. As the *Nottingham Journal* reported, 'as so often happens when a team is playing for time and not runs, wickets were soon going cheaply'. Nottinghamshire had to follow on, though they drew. Watchers didn't much care for it. Likewise at Edgbaston in June 1933, after Yorkshire made 449 for five on the first day, the *Birmingham Post* noted that Sellers 'did not show indecent haste in applying the closure'; Yorkshire batted on until 591 for six, their largest score since 1899. Again, Warwickshire had to follow on, but batted out the match. On such pitches favouring batsmen, Yorkshire might not force a win. That did not matter, because other teams might not win there either, and Yorkshire kept winning elsewhere.

On the field

*The championship-winning Derbyshire team of 1936.
Back row (l to r): Harry Elliott, Leslie Townsend, Bill Copson, H Parker (scorer),
Alf Pope, Denis Smith, Charlie Elliott. Seated: Harry Storer, Stan Worthington,
Arthur Richardson (captain), Tommy Mitchell, Albert Alderman.*

If Yorkshire needed runs in a hurry, they could make them. In August 1946 at Leicester, Yorkshire made 249 for five on the first day, that even Kilburn called 'uninspiring'. When Leicestershire just saved the follow-on, after rain, on the last morning Yorkshire scored 106 in 45 minutes (and 17 overs) so that Sellers could declare at lunch. Yorkshire did without the tea break, as the fielding side was allowed to, and the last Leicestershire pair hung on for 30 minutes.

As for batting against Yorkshire, Bill Edrich recalled in 1950 how it felt in 'the old days': 'There seem to be clutching hands all round you, and instead of pitting your wits against one man – the bowler – you are fighting the whole lot! Which is just as it should be.' Several fielders might stand close to the bat, almost within hand-shaking distance of the batsman. As an example of how only the strongest-willed could resist, at Sheffield in June 1937 the champions Derbyshire were 105 for seven at lunch on the first day. According to the *Bradford Telegraph and Argus*, the visiting captain Robin Buckston later looked a 'trifle foolish' when Sellers went to silly mid off, 'and Buckston fell straight into the trap of playing the ball tamely' into Sellers' hands off Verity. Such events, and the win by an innings, gave Yorkshire more than 15 points; it gave Derbyshire, and everyone else, a reminder. Sellers put it into words in January 1947 while he was reporting on the MCC in Australia: 'I am always a believer in the policy that once you have got your opponent down, keep 'em down and don't allow 'em to get up.' Whether Yorkshire batted or bowled first, they sought a lead in runs and the initiative, so as to apply more pressure when bowling again. Yorkshire never relented, even when it looked like it. At Bristol in July 1937, Yorkshire led on first innings by 60, then made 235 in the first two hours of the third day to set Gloucestershire 334. J.G.Coates in the *Bristol Evening World* noted afterwards that Sellers late on put on

Paul Gibb on to bowl 'rubbish' so that he could claim the new ball sooner. Sellers 'could afford to give away many runs whereas he dare not waste many minutes. That point did not appear to be generally recognised but [Monty] Cranfield [Gloucestershire's number ten] spotted it and played to defeat the ruse. Strategy plays an important part in cricket and A.B.Sellars [sic] has a pretty good knowledge of the finer points of captaincy.' Gibb in fact had Cranfield leg before and Gloucestershire lost just before 6 pm.

If the first few batsmen did well against Yorkshire, the later ones for many counties could not; and Yorkshire never gave up. More wickets might never be far away. Worcestershire in July 1934 for example lunched at 94 for two; then three wickets fell, including Bernard Quaife, run out by Sellers after answering a call late. In the return match a month later on a reportedly dead pitch at Bradford, Sidney Martin and Frank Warne defied Yorkshire for three hours after Worcestershire were ten for four. Sellers kept changing his six regular bowlers, then turned to Wilf Barber, who had only taken a couple of wickets in a season. First ball, Barber had Warne caught behind, and in his next over had the new bat Reg Perks stumped. Barber only bowled one more Championship over that summer. Even when you were doing well against Yorkshire, you had to beware. As the *Bristol Evening World* sports columnist Phil Barnes warned in June 1939 - after the first day's play, when Yorkshire were all out 176 and Gloucestershire well placed on 71 for one - 'You never know with Yorkshire'. They were resilient. *The Times* reckoned in June 1946: 'If ever there can be anything certain in cricket, the most variable of games, it is that a Yorkshire team is in its most dangerous mood when it is threatened with humiliation.' After Yorkshire were out for a mere 140 at Lord's, Middlesex were out for 74, including 'Compton snapped up sharply by Sellers at short-leg'. Yorkshire won by 73 runs, comfortably in a low-scoring match.

Wilf Barber and Brian Sellers.

Sellers turned first and often to Bill Bowes. In Sellers' eight years as captain before the Second World War, Bowes and Verity were the only two men always among the three who bowled most for Yorkshire in the Championship. Saturday 18 May 1946 at Canterbury was typical. After Yorkshire made 252 in 97.1 overs, Sellers kept Bowes bowling for 11 overs in the last 70 minutes of the day, as Kent slumped to 36 for five. *The Times* reported 'two superb catches at backward point by Sellers from crisp strokes by Sunnucks and Valentine', off Bowes. Then aged 37, Bowes was not as fast as in the 1930s when batsmen from most counties had to duck or be hit or be out when trying to avoid the ball – or all three, as at Chesterfield in May 1934 when Derbyshire captain Arthur Richardson tried to jump out of the way of a shoulder-high ball, and flung his bat to the ground, only for the ball to glance off his hand to Arthur Wood behind the wicket, alongside five slips. Such a definite field, and other evidence, suggests Bowes bowled as Sellers wanted. When Sellers saw Lindwall bowling bouncers in Australia in February 1947, he wrote: 'Whatever people may say, I think a bouncer is a fair ball, provided it isn't overdone. The batsman can either play it or leave it alone.' Sellers, like Jardine when defending bodyline, was cynically forgetting how such short balls – as they always have been and probably always will be – were a way of intimidating out lesser batsmen. At Worcester in July 1934, for instance, Reg Perks 'tapped up another bumper from Bowes' to give Sellers a simple catch at silly mid off. Sellers was also forgetting the gifted batsmen carried off the field hurt, such as Walter Keeton (hit on the left cheek at Nottingham in June 1933) and John Langridge (jaw, Hove, August 1932). Indeed, sometimes it sounded as if Bowes were bowling bodyline. During that Nottinghamshire match of June 1933, the *Nottingham Journal* wrote of Bowes bowling 'leg theory' and of Bill Voce – ironically, one of Jardine's bodyline bowlers – caught off Bowes in a 'leg trap', a field used by Bowes as late as 1939, according to newspapers.

Lord Hawke disapproved, as he told the county annual meeting in January 1935. If anyone in a Yorkshire cap bowled what Hawke termed 'direct attack', he hoped that 'our captain and every future captain' would do what he would have done – take the bowler off. Hawke evidently was not watching away matches. A story from Bill Edrich's 1950 memoir *Cricketing Days* suggested that Sellers relished how Bowes bowled. According to Edrich, Bowes and Edrich's captain Robins were having a feud. When Robins went in to bat, Sellers told Bowes: 'Get thee sweater on lad.' Verity bowled, then someone in Bowes' place, and when Robins was due to face the next over, Sellers said: 'Now Bill, take on at Hedley's end, now's thee chance!' Robins grinned, hit a couple of fours, was hit on the heart, and then caught; and the ill feeling was over. Edrich dated the affair to Lord's in 1937, except that Robins was only ever caught off Bowes at Sheffield that year. The story suggested Middlesex, who came second in those last four summers before the war, accepted how Yorkshire played. What of other players, spectators, and reporters?

Praise of Yorkshire was often sparing. Dour and uncompromising, the *Worcester Evening News* sports writer T.B.Duckworth called them when they were in the city in August 1935. Yorkshire did play that way, when they had to. At Chesterfield in August 1933, Derbyshire's spinners so tied down Sutcliffe and Sellers, they didn't score in the 15 minutes before lunch. When Sellers hit the last ball of the second over after lunch for three runs, cheers greeted what the ironic *Derby Evening Telegraph* called 'this very unusual enterprise'. Often, however, the other team was the slower scorer. In May 1937, on another batsman's pitch at Edgbaston, Yorkshire totalled 492 in 153.2 overs, pipped to first innings points by Warwickshire's 496 for eight, in 177 overs. T.B.Duckworth rightly pointed out Yorkshire's negatives ('their bowlers tend to send down so little bad length stuff') and positives ('quick decisive running' of singles that 'players of other counties would never dream of obtaining'). Under Sellers, Yorkshire played without sparkle - whatever that meant; they did what they had to, and no more, always keeping in mind that they had to keep going over a four-month season. Just as with Bradman, many observers reached for the same metaphor. E.W.Swanton watching Surrey fall to Bowes at The Oval in August 1932 marvelled at 'how such a wonderful machine as the Yorkshire side ever comes to be beaten'. By the end of that 595 for six at Edgbaston in 1933, the less impressed *Birmingham Post* felt 'one could respect the almost mechanical efficiency of the batsmen without being moved to enthusiasm by it'. At the dinner at the Savoy in London during the challenge match in September 1937, Bill Bowes sat next to Tuppy Owen-Smith of Middlesex who called Yorkshire's cricket soulless. The charge stuck with Bowes. 'Were we soulless?' he asked a dozen years later in his autobiography. He thought back also to when he missed seven weeks of 1937 thanks to an operation on his knee. In hospital in London he received 'the odd letter or so from Hedley Verity, Maurice Leyland and Herbert Sutcliffe' – in other words, none from his captain. Sellers did want to know him, but only as a fully fit bowler. Bowes recalled how at Bristol, one month after his return, Sellers said 'that he would recommend dropping me from the side if I did not do better'. Bowes asked: 'If I bust my knee for keeps will you take responsibility?' 'I'm only interested in performances,' Sellers answered.

In nine matches and 30 days after Bowes' return from a career-threatening injury, he had bowled 336.1 overs – so Sellers hardly gave him an easy recovery; and taken 35 wickets; hardly a failure. Those wickets however came every 57.6 balls, much worse than his career average of one wicket every 45.4. Significantly, in those eight Championship matches (the other was a draw against the New Zealand tourists) Yorkshire drew five and only won three. In the rest of that season, Yorkshire won 15, lost two and drew three. It was no coincidence; without Bowes at his best, Yorkshire were no champions. Bowes came good; so did Yorkshire. That exchange with Sellers rankled Bowes, as he admitted. Sellers had a point, but only with statistics, and 'performances' for Yorkshire – all abstractions; Bowes had a point about what was best for his body. In truth Bowes was not asking if he and his team had a soul; only if Sellers did.

Outsiders asked too, and with irony for Bowes. In May 1953, the satirical magazine *Punch* mocked the Yorkshire cricket team as stone-wallers, who

A near full house at North Marine Road, Scarborough, at 5 pm one 1930s summer. Note the markings for tennis courts in the outfield.

followed 'the Trueman doctrine – the remorseless harrying of opponents, terrorism true to the teachings of Lenin-Stalin-Bowes'. The satire on power politics of the Cold War was neat, likening the Yorkshire club to Communist Russia, and playing on the surname of the recent American president and the Yorkshire fast bowler. While *Punch* then was rather too obsessed about Communism, and cricket, for its own good, the metaphor did have meaning for Yorkshire; indeed ever since 1917, or Aristotle wrote Politics, it's been the profoundest question for any club or political body: what works best, tyranny or democracy? The Soviet Union or any tyranny claimed strength from its people working with one agreed purpose, whereas a capitalist democracy could never agree on policy. We know that the unity of the one-party state is a front; that a group always has at least two points of view, and that suppressing all ideas except the rulers' (who no doubt disagree among themselves) is unhealthy. So it was in the Yorkshire dressing room and around the committee table. Yorkshire had to pull off a trick that the Communist states of Sellers' time could not; giving people liberty so as to prosper, while preserving the tyranny. A cricketer, or a citizen, or a Communist economy, would wither if forever told what to do. Yet what if people used liberty to disagree with the tyranny? Would that be a signal to the tyrant to change - or to take away the liberty? And even if a tyrant ruled well, eventually he would have to retire. How would he like to choose a new one?

Plenty of evidence suggests that Sellers did have a soul. At Leicester in August 1938 Sellers was opening the batting on the second day with Arthur Mitchell. Onlooker of the *Leicester Evening Mail* claimed to see 'little sparkle about Yorkshire's batting ... it was mainly due to Sellers that the crowd of nearly 2000 had something to applaud'. In the years between the world wars, when so many in authority harped on about 'brighter cricket'

Gloucestershire at Scarborough, August 1934. While the visitors looked relatively ragged, they did beat Yorkshire by nine wickets. Photograph once owned by broadcaster John Arlott. Left to right: Denis Moore, Ces Dacre, Tom Goddard, Basil Allen, Charlie Parker, Bev Lyon, Reg Sinfield, Grahame Parker, Dallas Page, Billy Neale, Charlie Barnett.

(whatever that meant), they prized the amateur, above all as captain, who would play for the love of it. Even if it were true that all amateurs were good sports, and professionals bad, you could never generalise; the long season would grind everyone alike. Yet like all stereotypes, the one of the carefree amateur had some truth; why else did it last so long? As far back as 1904, Lord Hawke had written against an all-professional side and for some amateurs; the arguments were the same, but from different angles. Eleven professionals would 'only play for the gate', he said – that is, their wages – whereas amateurs were 'the moral backbone of a county team'. Only the amateur could afford to be selfless, to think not of his average or money but such intangibles as glory, beauty, and indeed morals.

Sellers could be, and sometimes was, daring. Against Middlesex at Sheffield in June 1932, after Yorkshire gained the first innings points by the end of the second day, Sellers reached 61 not out at lunch on the third, hitting Greville Stevens 'to long on and onto Spion Kop at square leg for four and six', as the *Sheffield Telegraph* reported. Sellers could have batted on towards a maiden century, to make his reputation. Instead he declared 141 ahead and 'went for the 100 to one chance' of bowling out Middlesex. Arthur Rhodes did take three early wickets, before Middlesex drew easily.

'Sellers could make a sporting gesture as bold and generous as anyone I have met,' said Hammond in one of his end of career memoirs. He singled out Bradford in May 1939. After a blank first day, Yorkshire took first innings points by the third morning. They then hit 162 in 21 overs and set Gloucestershire 189 in 100 minutes, which they made with a few minutes to spare. Some disapproved; 'results lose their virtue when there is a suspicion of artificiality in the contriving of them,' *The Times* sniffed the day after, as only it could. But all the players enjoyed it, Hammond recalled. At Sheffield on Tuesday 1 August 1933, after a blank second day, Yorkshire could only hope to lead Hampshire on first innings and take five points. They did while Leyland and Sellers put on 71 for the fifth wicket in 35 minutes, until Sellers - who admittedly only made 21 - skied a drive. Yorkshire could have batted carefully all day and saved themselves some fielding; instead they entertained the 5000 spectators. When Hampshire had to bat for the last 90 minutes, Sellers gave his regular bowlers less work by putting himself and Wilf Barber on. This was not dull, neither 'circus' nor 'cemetery' cricket, as Hammond said. By 1946, when Sellers had put his stamp on Yorkshire, given his record and that many of the players he inherited had retired, the notoriously careworn matches against Lancashire between the wars had become more purposeful. Hutton hooked the first ball at Manchester for four, and from 83 for five Frank Smailes and Sellers added 61; as Kilburn put it, 'a half volley was seen as a half volley'.

The best evidence that Sellers had a soul was the look of the man. At Manchester in 1938, Yorkshire at 285 for five were already 152 ahead when Sellers joined Leyland; Ronald Symond wrote in the *Daily Mail* how Sellers 'clouted Iddon for a mighty six to long on':

... and continued to lay on with relish. Though now in his 32nd year the Yorkshire captain still moves and bats with the characteristic angular movement of an outsize colt - all arms and legs ... obviously enjoying his fun at Lancashire's expense.

This was human, not 'mechanical efficiency'. As in any organisation with its own culture - the way it did things - Sellers was giving and taking at the same time; his words and deeds were influencing others and being influenced. Some things were out of his hands. To be the champion club - to repeat, the one that won most games - Yorkshire needed pitches with something for bowlers. When Arthur Sellers proposed the toast at the annual reunion lunch at Old Trafford in April 1932, he said:

Wickets have been prepared in recent years in a way that gives a bowler little chance ... there is no encouragement for the fast bowler. When the sun comes out after rain bowlers should come into their own but they often do not. We in Yorkshire have decided there shall be no undue preparation of wickets and we do not cover them. That means the bowler has an equal chance with the batsman.

Players saw it differently from the committee chairman. The Bradford wicket usually had 'some help for the seam bowler', Bowes wrote; 'there are few pitches in England so nasty', reckoned Bill Edrich. Sellers spoke more like his father: ' ... let us have more wickets where the bowler has a chance. Given natural wickets there is no need to talk about five day Tests, we shall finish them in less than four.' Although a batsman, given the choice Sellers took the bowlers' side. In a famous Roses match at Manchester in June 1933, Sellers won the toss, and chose to

Middlesex and England captain Walter Robins.

bat. Lancashire left-arm spinner Jack Iddon was soon bowling over the wicket into rough made by the opening bowler Frank Hodgson's boots. The patch made the ball do such strange things, Lancashire's captain Peter Eckersley left the field to suggest to Sellers that left-arm bowlers should only bowl around the wicket from the Stretford end. Sellers reportedly thanked Eckersley for the thought, but preferred that both sides should take their chance. Yorkshire ended the first day on 287 for five; 'the worst day's cricket I have ever seen', thundered 'Cricketer', Neville Cardus, in the *Manchester Guardian.* He only showed his ignorance of how well Yorkshire batted despite the rough (and Cardus said nothing about Eckersley's extraordinary offer, although as a critic he had plenty to say about a novel broadcast of music over loudspeakers). Sellers' 31 proved to be the third highest score of Yorkshire's 341, and indeed the match; for Macaulay and Verity spun out Lancashire for 93 and 92. Sellers gave another clue to his views before the 1937 end of season challenge match. Robins suggested a covered pitch. Sellers objected: 'On principle Yorkshire never cover wickets. They give the bowlers a chance.' In truth – as at Old Trafford in 1933 – Sellers meant uncovered wickets gave *his* two outstanding bowlers, Bowes and Verity, the better chance.

Besides the policies ruling the game, and the tactics during matches, Sellers enforced manners. As in other ways, Sellers could seem tyrannical to newcomers, and cast a shadow long after his time, yet Sellers was only applying a discipline – to himself and others - that men before him had set and willingly followed. In a 1951 article, Leyland urged Yorkshire cricketers to excel in the field: 'Try to keep an eye on the captain and obey him always (he has the responsibility).'

As a sign of how long Sellers' reputation lingered, in his 2013 memoir to mark his 80th birthday the umpire (and 1950s hopeful Yorkshire opener) Dickie Bird told a story about Arthur Booth, the left-arm spinner second to Verity in the 1930s (and who played alongside Sellers in the Yorkshire Second Eleven in 1931), who aged 43 became a main part of the Championship-winning side of 1946.

Arthur was stood talking to the crowd, hands in his pockets, while fielding on the edge of the boundary at Headingley, when one wag said to him: 'Better look out Arthur, he's watching thee, tha knows.'
'Who's watching me?'
'Sellers, who else,' came the reply. Arthur felt in his pocket, brought out a handkerchief and started blowing his nose. He then put it back in his pocket. At the end of the over, as he walked round the boundary edge, Sellers came up to him and said: 'It's a good job you had a handkerchief in your pocket, Arthur.' Never missed a trick, Mr Sellers.

This story has all the earthiness and meaning of a parable in the gospels: the quick thinking of Booth, knowing he had to pretend to have a reason to put his hands in his pockets; Sellers, who let Booth know he had seen (and understood) everything; and those watching, who were alive to everything as if it were theatre. As Booth presumably told the story against himself, that spoke of a community across generations, even while men inside the group were of differing rank; notice that the man in the crowd used Booth's first name - as a familiar, assuming they were of the same class - and Sellers' surname, implying social distance. Most telling of all was Bird's last line, the moral of the story, and that apparently casual, but in truth deeply felt, use of 'mister'. Poignantly, Bird was showing his respect for the older man, even long after his death, and although such things no longer mattered to many.

Sellers' last first class match, Scarborough festival against MCC, September 1948. Left to right: Coxon, Wardle, Brennan, Smailes, Yardley, Sellers, Lester, Hutton, Halliday, Wilson, Foord (looking rather detached). Contrast their neatness with the Gloucestershire team of 1934 on the same spot.

In two of the fullest and most insightful studies of Sellers, the batsmen Willie Watson and Ted Lester - who began under him - also gave the example of keeping hands out of pockets. Sellers insisted partly for the sake of appearances. Even if you were tired or hot, you never sat or lay on the field, when a batsman was out; that showed weakness and might give the new batsman confidence. Above all, because he was not a man who mistook style for substance, Sellers wanted his fielders alert for practical reasons: 'Often he would make discreet signals to his fielders. He would give the signal once. He would even give it twice, but never would he give it a third time. He would just wheel round on the fielder and roar at him,' Watson recalled.

Appearances, such as smartness in dress, mattered too because wherever

Yorkshire went, they were the main draw, and not only in the boom for all leisure after 1945. Long-serving players of other counties regularly chose the Yorkshire match for their benefit. Cricket then had a bigger place in English sport than since, and counties had a bigger place in English cricket. In August 1946, the biggest crowd at Leicester that season – an estimated 5000 – had to sit around a shortened boundary. This happened when Australia toured too; something else Yorkshire had in common with them. The local press took photographs, usually on the first day, either of the team taking the field, or the best-known players before play or at lunch, such as of Sellers and Alan Melville returning from the luncheon tent at Hove on Wednesday 28 August 1935, each man wearing a blazer (and Melville his pads as the not-out batsman). And everyone wanted Yorkshire autographs. While any cricketer may weary of the attention, Sellers at least sometimes obliged – which became another good news photograph. The *Leicester Evening Mail* in August 1938 for instance ran a picture of Sellers sitting on grass during an interval, and at least ten boys (some wearing school caps) around him. As the caption beneath explained, the 'besieged' Sellers 'found it handier to sit down to the task'. A year earlier, Sellers was standing in the middle before Yorkshire batted a second time, 'considering very intently what preparation the wicket required', the *Leicester Mercury* reported. Sellers hardly noticed the 'youthful autograph hunter': 'Groundsman White did however. He drove him off very much in the manner of an indignant gardener scaring away a flock of poultry from a newly sown flower garden.' At Chesterfield in July 1939, Sellers had less on his mind. On the Monday afternoon, of what proved a blank second day, Sellers and the Derbyshire captain Thomas Hounsfield were on their way to inspect the pitch, when 'Mr T Mycroft of Somercotes, son of the famous Derbyshire cricketer, continually clapped', so the *Derby Evening Telegraph* reported. 'Eventually Sellers turned around and beckoned to Mr Mycroft to accompany him on the inspection. Mr Mycroft did so and he was engaged in conversation with the two captains at the wicket for some time.' Whether Sellers did it to shut a critic up, or brighten his rain-ruined day, he was showing interest in the crowd. He was acknowledging that a county cricketer, let alone the Yorkshire captain, could not insist on privacy, on or off the field. Neither place was quite private, or public. The crowd might not spot Sellers' signals to move his fielders – and Sellers certainly did not want the batsmen to see – but the players on the field were there to be applauded, hooted at or judged like cattle at market. Off the field, privacy, even Masonic-like secrecy, was possible; except you were forever passing from private places into public; whatever you did might have public consequences. On the third day of that Australian tour match at Sheffield in 1938, Yorkshire needed only 67 with seven wickets in hand, when it began raining at lunch. At the last inspection at 4 pm, some disappointed spectators booed. A.G.Moyes wrote of how Sellers from the middle 'waved away the match':

He left the onlookers in no doubt. There was no secret conclave in the dressing-room and a subsequent whispering that this one or that had not wanted to continue. Sellers in his gesture was as definite as [umpire Frank]

Chester with his decisions. It seemed to me a sporting thing to do.

The difference between the public space of on the field and the private space off it became obvious when a batsman was out. In old age Sellers recalled:

It was very rare when the incoming batsman did not arrive in the pavilion that we did not have a discussion about what went wrong. We'd have a post-mortem nine times out of ten but *it wasn't resented because it was the same with us all – it was part of behaviour, nothing personal, purely constructive. We'd say, 'you know you played across that one, right across ...' it was communal self-help.*

That Sellers used the Latin 'after-death' shows how serious it can feel for a batsman to be out. Given that they were playing six days a week and might be out four times a week, one man could not upset the group with self-centred tantrums. And given the constant pressure for wins – a championship might turn on a single win or a draw – everyone, as Sellers understood, had to contribute to the improvement of all. Hence what Norman Yardley recalled as a 'bold experiment' in July 1939. Yardley was out of form and Yorkshire were third. Sellers proposed that Yardley would swap places with Sutcliffe and open at Northampton with Hutton. It had worked for Sellers when he began with four zeroes in 1935: 'never being afraid to take a risk, he promptly moved himself up in the batting order to number three' and made runs against Cambridge University. In each case, the batsman found form against weaker bowlers; the swapped batsman let himself be unsettled to do a good turn for another. Like any well-run group, the Yorkshire eleven - whoever they were on any day – set aside their different characters. They were, as Bowes recalled, 'at all times students of the game', whether on the field, or watching carefully off. On their second day at Oxford in May 1936, Yorkshire were all out for just after lunch for 356, a lead of 206. The *Oxford Mail* noticed that the Yorkshire players took a good look at a 'notorious spot' on the pitch: 'Verity could be seen rubbing his hands as if in joyful anticipation.' Anyone could see that gesture, and yet who could say for sure what it meant (were Verity's hands cold?). Who could tell what Verity, or anyone, was thinking? These men were on stage, and yet in private, at the same time.

Chapter Five
Off the field

All organized societies are cemented together, not merely by force and the threat of force, and by established patterns of institutional behaviour, but also by accepted ways of feeling and thinking and talking and looking at the world, by ideologies.
James Burnham, The Managerial Revolution (1945)

If the Yorkshire of Sellers, and before and after, had an ideology, it was of the county cap. It was more than a covering to keep your head warm and dry; when the club gave one to you, it was their sign that you belonged, because you were good enough to play regularly for them. You could, presumably, buy one, just as you could buy a Victoria Cross; but few could earn one. Fred Trueman buried his with his father.

If caps were so precious, why did the club give them with so little ceremony? John Nash gave Sellers his, as if it were a miner's lamp; a piece of kit. Thirty years later, John Hampshire felt 'utterly deflated' when asked to pick his out of a cardboard box. We can perhaps explain that because Yorkshire had a new captain, Brian Close, who had yet to make his mark. Sellers at least handed caps over; and, as he recalled it in old age, he included practical and long-term advice to the newly-arrived player:

I always gave the lads their county caps in the dressing - except Alec Coxon and I gave him his on the field; I took my own off and gave it him. I always told the lads - remember - look ahead ten years from now. Don't look down on anyone - whether they are threadbare or well dressed. Remember in ten years they'll be the bread and butter of your benefit.

Sellers was implying that the capped player would be there for enough years to make enough money to set himself up; left unsaid was what the player would have to do to stay in the team. As Coxon's crowning was public, we have accounts of it, that needless to say disagree. They agree it happened at Bradford in May 1947, against Sussex. According to Yardley, Yorkshire were batting when Coxon joined Sellers in the middle (in other words, Yardley could not have been beside them). Sellers beckoned, and when Coxon went to him, Sellers took off his cap and offered it. Sellers said: 'It's yours; congratulations, Alec!' and they shook hands. Johnny Wardle had Yorkshire fielding. Sellers had been off the field, at the committee meeting that decided on Coxon's cap.

When he came out he walked straight over to Alec and told him the glad news. Now it happened that there was no cap available on the Park Avenue ground and so eager to let the crowd know of Alec's success Sellers took off his own Yorkshire cap and placed it on the hero's head. It was one quarter applause and three-quarters uncontrollable mirth. The cap was several sizes too big and blotted out Alec's face like a candle snuffer.

Whichever story was correct, Sellers understood that the cap mattered to a player; and those watching. How can we explain, though, the usual hand-over, without ceremony or warmth, as Wardle described his? 'Brian Sellers called me over in the pavilion, announced sternly that he had some information to give me, and then told me without a smile that the committee had come to a certain conclusion about me. At that he shoved a cap into my hands and rumbled his congratulations.' This was the club's way – as faithfully carried out by Sellers – of managing a contradiction. Most employers, as we know well, care little for their workers; certainly few Yorkshire mines or factories in Sellers' time did. The county cricket club was an exception; its caps publicly honoured, for life, a handful of men. Honouring miners and factory workers was what Stalin's Soviet Union did. The only way to get round that in England – recognising working men as excellent, while keeping them down economically – was to hand out the cap as coldly as possible, to keep the wearers in their place; to make sure (an especially appropriate metaphor here) they did not become big-headed.

We have far less evidence about what Sellers did off the field. Jim Kilburn and other Yorkshire reporters that followed the team were welcome to

*A 1936 team picture at Harrogate.
Standing (l to r): Bright Heyhirst, Wilf Barber, Cyril Turner, Arthur Mitchell, Len Hutton, Hedley Verity, Bill Bowes, Frank Smailes, William Ringrose, Joseph Johnson. Seated: Arthur Wood, Herbert Sutcliffe, Brian Sellers, Paul Gibb, Maurice Leyland.*

enter the dressing room, but like all journalists, they had to trade access for discretion. The players might have felt embarrassed if dressing room affairs became public. If a journalist reported anything they saw or heard inside the dressing room, the players would lose their privacy; they would not be able to trust the journalists, or each other. It was not worth a journalist losing that trust for the sake of one story, however revealing. Willie Watson for instance in his 1956 autobiography recalled how he cowered when Sellers told Hutton off for arriving less than an hour before a match. By then, Hutton was about retired; and Watson in any case left Yorkshire for Leicestershire in 1958. Was the autobiography, that was bound to be too indiscreet for someone, a cause of Watson leaving; or a sign that he was too independently-minded to stay happily at Yorkshire much longer? Telling tales of the dressing room broke a taboo; and if you did it in a book, were you doing it all the time, in conversation? As late as 2014, Geoffrey Boycott – one of the youngest players to experience Sellers – described how the culture in his playing career was 'to keep everything within the dressing room'. It made sense; if you told your opponents anything, it might give them heart, or they might use it against you. Boycott added: 'We all knew deep down that if you betrayed that trust, the chairman of Yorkshire, Brian Sellers, would sack you.' Such a culture was all the more powerful because it was 'deep down', unwritten and unspoken; self-imposed.

Warwickshire and England captain Bob Wyatt.

At 11.50 am on Friday 14 June 1935 at Edgbaston, Yorkshire began batting; they had 40 minutes before lunch, and then the last four hours of the match, to make 315 to win. That they made 225 for three after 87 overs might suggest they chose to draw, for three points; rather than risk defeat, and none. As the *Birmingham Post* put it the next day, 'the path of safety was preferred'. Dour Yorkshire? As so often, the truth was in the detail. Sutcliffe began briskly, clearly 'inspired by a determination to strive for victory', as the *Post* reported; only he was bowled for 24 out of 27 just before lunch. Hutton, the other opener, retired on 17 at 59, 'far from well'. Nor could Yorkshire do as they pleased; the Warwickshire captain Bob Wyatt set his field to keep run-making down, and his bowlers bowled wide of the off stump (who was not playing 'bright' cricket?!). From what happened on the field, we can guess that off the field Yorkshire agreed a plan; they began by trying to win, and once it became too risky to keep up with the clock, only then did they indeed prefer safety. Just as batsmen had to adapt, to the state of a match, so the captain had a balancing act. He had to keep the confidence of his men by staying in control, and being seen to have control; except that by the rules of the game, batsmen when on the field were on their own. On that Friday at Edgbaston, Sellers only went out to bat at the end, and was one not out. And what made life harder for Sellers, to repeat, was that he never reached the team on merit.

He had to keep the final say on decisions to himself, and he had to impose himself to earn it; hence that crucial confrontation off the field at Oxford in 1932. Paradoxically, once he had authority, he was most likely to be successful, and so keep his power, by seeking advice. For example, Sellers reportedly consulted Sutcliffe and Verity before he declared overnight at Hull in July 1934, leaving Essex the last day to make 255. As Yorkshire won by 123 runs, the decision might look correct and simple. The *Sheffield Daily Telegraph* called it 'very sporting'. If Sellers had batted on, and given Essex less time to make more runs, Yorkshire would have made it harder to lose; but also to win, as they had less time to take ten wickets. The captain forever had to balance; opposition batsmen against his bowlers, the pros and cons of practical jokes – 'the good captain must see that they are kept within reasonable bounds, or else his team will go to pieces', Hammond advised – and the well-being of his ten men, who off the field were as frail as anyone else. A captain had to know who to turn to, because it was as foolish to ask the ignorant for advice as it was to ignore the wisest; not only then would the captain have poor advice, but the team would see that the captain did not know his men. It made sense for the captain to turn to some men more than others; yet he could not have – nor be seen to have – favourites; others would resent that, and the team would no longer be united. Often Sellers had to be decisive; if any captain took too long to declare, that in itself was a decision not to declare, and it made a draw ever more likely. Yorkshire folk had long memories: when the *Yorkshire Evening Post* announced in August 1946 that Sellers would report for it from Australia on that winter's MCC tour of Australia, it made a neat pun: 'Sellers has never lacked courage in his decisions on the field – he put the 1938 Australians in to bat at Sheffield and got desperately near to beating them – and he has never lacked courage in his declarations when talking off the field of the game.'

Sussex all-rounder Jim Parks.

Other decisions spoke of the team's culture, that Sellers, the leader, was only expressing. It may seem extraordinary that county cricketers played on Friday 1 September 1939, the day that Germany invaded Poland; in fairness, Britain only declared war on the Sunday, an extraordinary wait in hindsight. Yorkshire were already champions. As newspapers reported, that Friday morning, the Yorkshire club suggested cutting short their match at Hove. Sellers replied 'that his team would prefer to play it out as the game had been set aside for the benefit of Jim Parks', of Sussex. In his memoir *Thanks to Cricket*, Jim Kilburn wrote of 'an impromptu team meeting'. Whether Kilburn heard it first hand or second, Sellers said: 'We are public entertainers, and until we have instructions to the contrary we carry on as usual.' Whenever Sellers made the decision – Kilburn implied it happened sooner than the Friday morning, perhaps even before the match – and for whatever reason, Sellers was thinking of others than himself and his men: whether the paying public ('the bread and butter of your benefit') or a fellow professional seeking money for his benefit. By doing others a good turn, Yorkshire could reasonably hope for good in return. Kilburn went on simply and movingly to describe how Yorkshire took the first innings lead and the match – as true professionals – and took a coach to Leeds. 'Goodbyes were brief and dispersal was without ceremony.' Perhaps Sellers' lack of ceremony when giving a county cap was only part of a deeper masculine culture of leaving even the deepest emotion best unsaid. For on 1 September 1939, as Kilburn wrote: 'Not a cricket season, but a cricket era was over.'

How Yorkshire behaved on the outbreak of world war was only how they behaved usually. At Leicester in August 1946, Yorkshire players carried around collection boxes for Norman Armstrong; at Hove in 1934, Sellers officiated at the raffle for Tich Cornford's benefit. In August 1947, Sellers unusually chose not to make Worcestershire follow on, though Yorkshire led by 247 on first innings (and in their eventual second innings Worcestershire only made 132). According to the *Worcester Times and News*, 'this gesture was presumably for Perks' benefit', as Reg Perks had chosen the match for his benefit. As Sellers' three main bowlers were either in their late 30s (Bowes and Robinson) or in only their third full month of county cricket (Wardle), Sellers may have had in mind only a rest for his team, so late in the season, knowing that a win would be no less likely. At least it did not seem ridiculous to print that Sellers might bat again, to prolong a match so that more people paid to watch. Perhaps Sellers only thought of winning all along. At Scarborough in August 1939, in the same position, almost to the run, Sellers did the same. 'To the majority of people his policy was inexplicable', the *Birmingham Post* said; it speculated that Sellers felt the pitch would wear more to suit his spinners even more. Sellers declared after only 33 overs, when Yardley was 83 not out, having made 108 in the first innings; Sellers evidently closed an innings when it suited him and the team, and did not allow batsmen even a few extra minutes to reach a milestone. Such a prompt decision served more than one purpose. Besides making the win more likely – and Warwickshire were only out the next day with 25 minutes (and the extra half hour) to spare – it told the world, and reminded the players, that to Yorkshire winning mattered above all. Only 36 days before, Sellers had let Yardley open against weak Northamptonshire, so that he could find form; as he had. Again, Kilburn best explained Yorkshire cricket. The county did best – under Lord Hawke, then Sellers, then Close – when players were not allowed to be satisfied with themselves. Playing for Yorkshire, let alone captaining it, was not an end in itself. Kilburn wrote in old age in 1975: 'Sellers and his players constructed a close community of ideals and interests'; an ideology, to use a word popular in the 1930s, when communism and fascism were all the rage.

In the style of the lifelong newspaper reporter that he was, Kilburn summed up: 'The self-discipline of the Sellers era avoided criticism perhaps because it had not become oppressive when cricket was interrupted.' Kilburn might have lightened his style by telling a story, giving an example (why was discipline under Sellers not oppressive? and was Kilburn implying it became oppressive after 1945?). Sellers did give some clues while he was writing for the *Yorkshire Evening Post*. On his return to England on Wednesday evening, 19 March 1947, he told well-wishers how he longed to be in action with a Yorkshire team again: 'It will be grand to be with the lads again on English turf.' Sellers, had just turned 40, was far from the only cricketer, then or since, to call his fellow players 'lads'. It suggested the captain – or rather the less formal 'skipper' – was one of those 'lads', familiar, even juvenile. Like other groups, the 'lads' had their own words, which served to bind the group together, and kept out everyone else who did not understand. Again, thanks to Sellers' months as a newspaper correspondent, we know a few of those words, otherwise lost in the air of the dressing room. The *Yorkshire Evening Post's* diary column in November 1946 pointed out that Sellers used such language to describe an innings of Hutton; it was a 'jaffa':

To the Yorkshire players anything that is a jaffa is just about as good as it can be and anything that is sawdust is right at the other end of the scale. A poor thing which should not have happened. A jaffa of a ball because bigger than other oranges and sawdust of no use to anyone.

Sadly, most of those private words are as lost to us as the reasons why men built Stonehenge. We have one more, again from when Sellers arrived in Poole Harbour by flying boat. 'Little John' of the *Yorkshire Evening Post* reported: '... for those who had gone out in the tender to meet him there was the old cheerful 'shabash' heard so often in happy and successful times in the Yorkshire dressing room.' Shabash is Urdu for 'bravo', a sign of how words from the British Empire entered the English language. Jaffa as a word has stuck, at least inside cricket; sawdust and shabash have not. The words had meaning only to Sellers and his men, the same as their nicknames. Again, Yorkshire were not the only team to revel in nicknames; any short man was 'Tich' for instance. That there were so many nicknames under Sellers told of men at home with one another: 'Tiddly' Barber; 'Ticker' Mitchell. Kilburn suggested that Sellers liked such names: "... 'Timber' [Wood] was scarcely avoidable in a dressing room infected by the uninhibited A.B.Sellers". As Kilburn explained, Sellers was 'Skipper' inside the dressing room. That neatly honoured the office of captain, the same as a football manager was 'Gaffer', while allowing for the fact that the holder of the office kept changing. Otherwise, Sellers was nicknamed 'Cracker', short for Crackerjack, 'in retort to repeated insistence that Yorkshire were the crackerjacks of county cricket'. Such slang is hard to pin down at the time, let alone later, because each era has its own. A cracker-jack was an excellent person or thing, a maestro; we might say 'the bees' knees', or 'champion'. From the northern slang word 'crackers', and the BBC TV children's show (after Sellers' time as a player), we might also think of a crackerjack as mad or zany. Slang words might mean nothing, or start with meaning forgotten with time, and be said for the shared sheer nonsense.

Whatever Sellers meant, the name 'crackerjack' fitted him and his team. If he was hinting at craziness, it was for a reason; a team had to stand out from normal people, to come first.

Much of the evidence of Sellers as an off the field character came when he had a pint in hand. He recalled in old age:

.... we met the other players, knew the opposition lads. And I got to know those that could take their ale like men and do their stuff; others who had a few and wouldn't be able to do much before lunch because they couldn't take it like men. You know, when you bend down you see stars, that stuff. So I would say to them, 'OK we've all done it. So steady on.' Never had any trouble.

In an age when we frown on drinking in working hours and driving when drunk, it's significant that Sellers – who threatened to drop Bowes for not taking wickets fast enough – condoned men who, at least sometimes, were hung over the next morning. Also significant is this idea of being 'like men'; to drink beer was masculine. Police caught Ellis Robinson in 1947 driving home, so drunk he could hardly stand; we might wonder how many more cricketers did the same, and how often. By having a drink after play, you belonged; but just as there was a limit to how much a man could stomach, there was a limit to how much noncomformity Sellers could stomach. In his 1987 autobiography, Boycott told of 'an incident' after he made 126 not out against Cumberland at Gargrave, in front of Sellers. It was Wednesday evening, 23 May 1963. Boycott was 21:

We went into a pub and Sellers offered to buy a round. When it came to my turn and I told him I would like an orange juice he snorted with contempt. 'You can buy your own bloody orange juice. Fancy drinking orange juice ...' I didn't know Sellers well at the time, though his power at Yorkshire was legendary and he was obviously a man used to giving orders and having his own way. There was no need for him to try and belittle a young man who quite simply did not like the taste of beer. I felt small and humiliated.

In 2014, Boycott told a similar story, and sounded more understanding: 'That was the culture. Brian was not a bad man but he thought if you had a drink it would solve everything. It was a very macho approach.' That the older Boycott used the term 'culture' is a sign of how we are analysing sport ever more, treating sport as an occupation like any other, teams as organisations, and fields of play as workplaces. A risk is always that we load our perspective on the past, when men did not think in ways we do. Another is that we forget, or deride, what was once normal. In 1962, and when Sellers began with Yorkshire 30 years before, talk after work 'over a pint' among workmates was normal, and not only among cricketers. Yet not everyone does what's normal. In old age Sellers said: 'Some of the lads, of course, forever tripping the light fantastic, others went to a film, others they'd all join up together and talk – cricket.' Sellers had evidently forgotten by Boycott's time that not everyone had chosen to stand at the bar, and they had been free to do other things. The tragedy for Yorkshire cricket, after Sellers hurt Boycott, was manifold: why did Sellers not allow a young man to be cricket-mad and teetotal? Why did Boycott not accept a half, just to be social? Or perhaps the tragedy was cultural, and everyone's fault; that men (and never mind women) could not have a good time in a pub unless they boozed.

Sellers could be a more thoughtful host. The Surrey captain Errol Holmes in his memoir, *Flannelled Foolishness*, described Sellers as 'a typical Yorkshire man with sparking wit and yet iron determination':

He shook me warmly by the hand, told me that he was glad to see me, and that Yorkshire were out to give Surrey a good walloping and then announced that I was staying with him for the match. That evening I met his delightful wife Bright and had Sunday lunch next day; I had Yorkshire pudding as only they can make it and serve it in Yorkshire on a plate by itself and covered with gravy.

Whereas Sellers left so many traces to do with cricket, he left little about his home and his life outside cricket. That cannot have been accidental; it was none of our business. An exception is his wedding, in October 1932. George Macaulay, Wilf Barber, Arthur Wood and the bowlers Frank Dennis and Arthur Rhodes and scorer William Ringrose attended the ceremony at Saltaire Methodist Church; Sutcliffe, Leyland, Bowes and Verity on their way to bodyline sent a telegram. The bride, the daughter of a Bradford chartered accountant, was Bessie Walker: 'He called her Bright-eyes,' their daughter-in-law Anne Sellers recalled.

Brian Sellers and Bessie Walker, before their wedding.

Chapter Six
Batsman, fielder, bowler – and England captain?

> *Cricket is a team game in which the individual, nevertheless, at intervals and in his turn, is called upon to assert and exploit his individuality, without ever forgetting his obligation to the team. I hope that does not sound confusing or contradictory.*
> Lionel, Lord Tennyson, Sticky Wickets (1950)

Learie Constantine left as long and vivid a picture in words as any of what it was like for a batsman and bowler to face Sellers. At Harrogate in July 1939, Yorkshire were well behind the West Indies on first innings when Sellers walked out to bat, 'jauntily swinging his bat' to acknowledge applause. He told Constantine: 'I am going to beat the guts out of those little slows of yours today, Learie! Better let someone else take a turn.' Constantine grinned, "for we had a standing engagement for battle after some friendly frictions in the past, and told him 'not today, not on your life'. I believe I bowled him with the second ball of my next over ..."

When Constantine came in to bat again, Sellers asked what he was going to do:

I said, you will see, Sellers! And the first ball that was sent up to me I drove at him with force enough to have gone clean through him and out the other side – and halfway to Sheffield after it! He got his hands to it and stopped it somehow and I will bet he would have given brass to be able to wring his hands to take the pain out of them, but he only grinned at me and I knew if I did it again somehow he would defy every law of ballistics and catch me out. I need not have worried because I was out a couple of balls later in any case but as I left he added fuel to the fire by saying, 'didn't you dare to give me another?'

Note again the difference between Constantine more respectfully using the captain's surname and Sellers using the player's first name. Rain next day denied the tourists a likely win. Sellers laughed and said, 'now you know why God is a Yorkshireman'. After such a full playing career, Constantine's memory was at fault - in fact Bertie Clarke bowled Sellers (another example of Sellers getting out to a spinner). Constantine had however captured the authentic Sellers: physically hard; priding himself on not showing pain, even though he felt it like anyone else; a chatty, assertive homo ludens. Sellers was like that from the start. In January 1933 he opened an 'at home' at Barnoldswick cricket club, inside Lancashire but near Keighley. He gave his two penn'orth about bodyline. He had no sympathy for the Australians: 'I think it is a question of the boot on the other leg and they don't like it. Yorkshire have had a lot of this kind of bowling to play against especially when we were playing Nottinghamshire but you never found Yorkshire squealing.'

None of this necessarily made him very successful at batting. In his 1941 sketch, Robertson-Glasgow called him 'no more than a good batsman':

... strong, tall, long in the reach, a stubborn or violent number six according to need; but as a fielder, especially in the close positions, he is often brilliant. His bowling, I have heard him say, has distinct possibilities, never fully appreciated or developed by the captain.

Again – and Robertson-Glasgow left his readers to appreciate it – Sellers was telling a joke against himself, as he was the captain that never bowled himself enough. That touched on the problem for every captain; even if you had skills as a leader, you had to justify yourself as a cricketer. Like any batsman, he scored unevenly. He averaged 23 for Yorkshire. He did poorly in London, averaging only 17 at The Oval and 14 at Lord's; yet he averaged 26.4 against Middlesex. Did playing away make a difference? Again, there seemed no pattern; at Manchester he averaged 45, which was nearer his home than Chesterfield, where he averaged only 12; and both were nearer him than Scarborough, where he averaged under 21. Derbyshire in that era excelled in seam bowlers; except that half the time at Chesterfield, the leg-spinner Tommy Mitchell got Sellers out. So it was around the counties for all his career. When Sellers made that 61 not out at Bramall Lane in June 1932, the *Sheffield Daily Telegraph* reported that 'his judgement was at fault occasionally especially when he grew over-confident in playing [Jim] Sims' leg breaks'. At Lord's against MCC in 1937, Sellers 'tried to hit Robins over Father Time', and was stumped. And at Sheffield in June 1946 Sellers played to the pitch of the ball on the off, 'but it swept around his legs to knock back his leg stump', and Sellers was bowled for three by the 48-year-old Johnny Clay (his fingers 'still packed with cunning').

In an age when many counties had leg-spinners, this weakness of Sellers – in Kilburn's verdict, 'he tended to play spin bowling after the manner of submarine navigation – by guess and by God' – could have been crippling. Sellers managed; he averaged nearly 28 against Warwickshire, for instance, despite Eric Hollies and George Paine; and 26 against Kent, despite Tich Freeman and then Doug Wright. Reporters and no doubt players noticed. At Sheffield in July 1937, the Middlesex leg-spinner Tuppy Owen-Smith caught and bowled him. 'I still think he would do better to go down the pitch to them and chance his keen eye and powerful shoulders,' the *Sheffield Telegraph* reckoned. Even in 1951, playing for Yorkshire 'old masters' in a charity match at Headingley, Sellers was caught for one off the leg-spinner Eddie Leadbeater, trying to force runs. Defending or attacking made no difference. He 'jumped out to Mitchell' at Chesterfield in June 1936, 'changed his mind and gave the bowler a simple return', the *Derby Telegraph* reported. In fairness, Sellers was far from alone; Yorkshire followed on that day. As with the world-beating Australian team around the year 2000, Sellers and other batsmen of Yorkshire's lower order might have to seek quick runs after the first batters had done most of the work, or they had to try to repair a broken innings. In either case, Sellers was likely to be soon out, which would lower his average. Even a few runs might do for the team, as at Chesterfield in July 1938. Sellers had been second top scorer in Yorkshire's first innings, and went in at eight on the third day, wanting to declare. Sellers' rapid 13 included what the *Derby Telegraph* called 'a delightful sweep to leg' off Mitchell, before Denis Smith at slip caught Sellers off a slash that glanced off wicket-keeper Harry Elliott's pad. In the scorebook it looked a failure; except Yorkshire won.

To compensate, Sellers and others could make easier runs off tired bowlers, and according to many match reports when Yorkshire batted first, their 'brightest' batting came late in the day.

Brian Sellers batting in the nets.

Some bowling was too good for most. Sellers was 'completely at sea' against Maurice Tate at Hove in August 1932, and 'it was no surprise' to the *Sussex Daily News* that Sellers played inside an off break and was bowled for eight – the same score and dismissal as Sutcliffe's that morning. It was no coincidence that Sellers made his career highest score in May 1936 not against a county but the weaker Cambridge University. Norman Yardley, then a student playing for Cambridge, noted in his memoir that 'several of our best men were absent' for exams, including the opening bowler Wilf Wooller. Sellers promoted himself to three; Sutcliffe went in at four and made 49, and the two made 177 in two and a quarter hours, which to the *Cambridge Daily News* was slow. Sellers gave two hard chances behind the wicket before his century, and an easy one to the captain Hugh Bartlett at 164. Sellers ended the day on 192 not out, having made 98 since tea. On the second, colder day, some knowing spectators applauded Sellers on 195, as that was the highest score by a Yorkshire amateur. He was caught at first slip off the new ball for 204, in five hours, having hit one six and 25 fours; 'not without blemish' according to the Cambridge newspaper, but 'powerful'. The next morning, a 'mysterious parcel' arrived at Fenner's. The headmaster of Sellers' and Yardley's old school, Stanley Toyne, a well-read man who was a good enough cricketer to play once for his native Hampshire (against Yorkshire), had sent two miniature bats with messages of congratulation. As so often after an outstanding innings, Sellers slumped; in June he made 146 runs at 13, and 101 at 10.1 in July. He ended 1936 with fewer runs than the season before or after. *The Cricketer* magazine summed it up as 'disappointing'.

Sellers' first century against a county came at Nottingham in July 1937, 'a really great innings' according to *The Times*. Harold Larwood and Bill Voce had taken the first four wickets for 50. Off a short run, Larwood was bowling at a pace 'approaching that of his erstwhile great days', the *Nottingham Journal* gushed. Many of Sellers' runs came off snicks; which was forgivable against Larwood and Voce, in ever poorer light. A sharp shower at 3.40 pm held up play for 40 minutes, which gave the fast men a rest. Voce bowled Smailes - who made the next highest score, 20 - and Wood, and Yorkshire at 138 for seven still needed 39 to make Nottinghamshire bat again. As so often, dropped catches - two in two balls by Larwood, off Verity and Sellers - made all the difference. Verity was bowled exactly 150 behind, and Ellis Robinson saved the follow-on.

*Brian Sellers batting against Kent in 1938;
the picture was signed by him and the slip fielder, Arthur Fagg.*

Having rescued Yorkshire, Sellers – 'who more than any other captain seems able to make runs when they are urgently necessary', the *Manchester Guardian* said – gambled when on 89, as the last man Bowes was a notoriously bad bat. Sellers hit Harold Butler to leg for six, out of the ground. As that brought up the 200, Nottinghamshire could take the new ball anyway. Sellers hit another six to leg to take him to 101, and was 103 not out of 209 when Bowes was run out.

Arguably Sellers' finest innings was in July 1934, at Sheffield against the Australians. Sellers won the toss and chose to bat on a soft pitch that took plenty of sawdust ('it presented the appearance of a strip of ground undergoing intensive horticulture', C.L.R.James wrote in the *Manchester Guardian*). Sellers entered at 149 for four when Hans Ebeling bowled Cyril Turner for ten; and Ebeling almost bowled Sellers first ball. He and Smailes 'weathered [Clarrie] Grimmett, then hit him' and added 74 at better than a run a minute. Sellers ended the Saturday 49 not out of 238 for six. In the first over on the Monday Grimmett bowled Smailes round his legs. The Australian bowling never bothered Sellers, C.L.R.James wrote:

He shoved Grimmett round to fine leg, dashed out unexpectedly twice and smashed him to the boundary twice; he cut Wall through the slips to the boundary, in the nineties he stepped back to Ebeling's half-volley and drove it for four past cover's hand. At 99 he ran out rather recklessly to Fleetwood-Smith, but made everybody happy by hitting him to fine leg for four. His cricket was sound, polished and vigorous, and after Wall bowled him he had a great reception ....

However, Bradman overshadowed Sellers. He came in at 16 for one, wearing a sweater despite sunshine, and made 140 of the next 189 in less than two hours. After a sketchy first quarter of an hour, his second 50 came in 23 minutes, the last 40 in 20. 'No living batsman and few dead ones could surpass the ease, the variety and the power of the 22 fours and two sixes,' C.L.R.James wrote. In the second innings, Sellers made only 13, but added 58 with the stand-in opener Wood, as Yorkshire batted long enough for a draw.

Bradman also impressed as a fielder; as did Sellers. Bob Wyatt in his staccato way summed up Sellers well in his 1939 book *The Ins and Outs of Cricket*: 'A magnificent fielder, usually seen at cover point. His speedy and accurate throwing saves many runs. Always sets a fine example in the field.' In a 1982 collection, *County Champions*, Duncan Kyle recalled seeing Sellers, with 'that sailor's gait of his', leading Yorkshire down the steps at Bradford in 1946:

... grinning and hurling the ball jokily at Arthur Wood from a range of about five feet, and Wood, with his trencherman's shape and his fox-terrier reflexes, taking it sweetly and flicking it back, and the crowd delighted and relieved to see that these were still the same men;

after six summers of war. Again, Yorkshire resembled the Australians by insisting on good fielding. That throwing around of the ball, as the Australians did, prepared everyone, cemented a symbolic and practical

Batsman, fielder, bowler – and England captain?

The 1934 Australian tourists.
Standing (l to r): William Ferguson (scorer), Bill Brown, Ernest Bromley, Tim Wall, H Bushby (manager), Bill O'Reilly, Leslie Fleetwood-Smith, Len Darling, Clarrie Grimmett, William Bull (treasurer). Sitting: Hans Ebeling, Arthur Chipperfield, Don Bradman, Bill Woodfull, Alan Kippax, Stan McCabe, Bert Oldfield. Front: Ben Barnett, Bill Ponsford.

A signed picture of Sellers and Arthur Wood going out to bat for Yorkshire against MCC at Scarborough in September 1933.

67

bond between players, and was a burst of playfulness. Sellers was as at home 'scouting' in the deep as ready to snatch the ball almost off the bat. While 21st century fielding in general may well be better than in previous centuries, Sellers was surely as skilful as anyone. At Hove on Wednesday 26 August 1936 - a remarkable day as Sellers bowled 12 overs, more than he bowled in most seasons - Jim Parks was first out, when he played to cover for a single, 'but A.B.Sellers speedily fielded the ball and registered a direct hit'. As with tactics and team culture, Sellers was not pioneering, merely joining other outstanding fielders, one generation among others before and since. That contemporary-sounding, indeed clichéd, phrase 'it is *catches* that win *matches'* came from Lord Hawke in 1904.

Just as number elevens are overly, even amusingly, proud of their batting, so Sellers was more of a bowler than his first-class career total of nine wickets might suggest. For Keighley he was a fifth or sixth bowler; which for league cricket was very occasional, as a couple of professionals might do much of the bowling. He did most in 1933, when he bowled the ninth-most overs for Yorkshire in the County Championship. At Leyton in mid-July he opened the bowling in the first innings with Macaulay - for a single over, then Verity came on. Against Middlesex in the next match at Bradford he took two tail-end wickets for ten, his best first-class figures. That was enough for the *Yorkshire Post* to talk up Sellers as likely to open the bowling with Arthur Rhodes at Bournemouth: 'Sellers has a natural ability to make the ball swing away and there are those who have watched him closely who say that with the necessary experience and practice he ought to become a new ball bowler of some merit.' In fact two reserves, Charles Hall and Cyril Turner, opened the bowling; Sellers came on first change and took one for 19 in five overs. Meanwhile Sellers' main three bowlers Verity, Macaulay and Bowes, besides Sutcliffe, were among the 12 for the second Test against the West Indies at Manchester. Again as first change Sellers only bowled six overs, out of 134, in the second innings, and only bowled eight overs in the next match, when his main bowlers were back. Such detail shows that Sellers only bowled to fill a hole. In the New Zealanders' second innings at Headingley in July 1937, Sellers as the eighth bowler had figures of two overs for one run; which hid the four balls he sent to the boundary for 16 byes, so that the total passed 200 and he could claim a new ball, a trick that almost worked as two more wickets fell and the tourists drew with nine men out. The same trick worked at Headingley in July 1936. Yorkshire beat Surrey by an innings and 185 runs - which sounded an easy win; yet at 3 pm on the last day, when the umpires would draw stumps at 4.30 pm, Surrey only had five wickets down. Sellers bowled what *The Times* termed one 'distinctly original', maiden over, that included nine wides and four byes. Bowes and Smailes took the new ball and the last five wickets for five runs. While Sellers was not much of a bowler, he at least proved that he lacked vanity.

Sellers soon made a name for himself. A stalwart of *The Cricketer*, Sir Home Gordon, named Sellers as captain of an 'interesting side of newcomers' in the magazine's annual for the 1932-3 winter. In his first winter as county captain Sellers showed himself a willing and opinionated public speaker

The 1939 West Indies tourists.
Standing (l to r): Fergie Ferguson (scorer), Gerry Gomez, Jeffrey Stollmeyer, Leslie Hylton, Tyrell Johnson, Bertie Clarke, Peter Bayley, Foffie Williams.
Sitting: George Headley, Ivan Barrow, Rolph Grant (captain).
JM Kidney (manager), John Cameron, Learie Constantine, Manny Martindale.
Front: Kenneth Weekes, Derek Sealey, Vic Stollmeyer.

Glamorgan captain Maurice Turnbull.

at the usual round of club and league dinners, claiming for instance that the Australians were 'flaid to death' of bodyline. Even his use of dialect was a sign of confidence. County cricket then, like the country, was not quick to bring on the young. Sir Home Gordon had said of his 'newcomers' that 'three or four years hence some of these should prove themselves more than competent'. That within four years Sellers was a genuine candidate as captain of England said as much about the lack of other options as about his own rise. Column-writers agreed that fewer amateurs were around with enough talent and experience to lead England. Only moral and class prejudice kept a professional cricketer from captaining his country, just as only sentiment long stopped Yorkshire choosing men born outside the county, and patriots later howled at a foreigner managing the England football team.

Arthur Carr, himself a former England captain, in May 1934 listed six men as in the running for the captaincy against Australia: Percy Chapman (the ageing Kent captain), Bob Wyatt (captain in four Tests), Cyril Walters (captain for the first Test, who significantly Carr slighted as 'hardly strong enough in his control over professionals to be seriously considered'), two county captains Maurice Turnbull (Glamorgan) and Bev Lyon (Gloucestershire), and Bryan Valentine, (playing under Chapman and only

Kent captain Bryan Valentine.

Kent captain after the war). While Sellers was not on Carr's list in 1934, by 1936 he was a contender. Yorkshire newspapers at least were calling Sellers the best man for the job. In July 1937, Looker-on in the *Sheffield Telegraph* said: '...if his batting last season had been more consistent he would probably have been chosen to make the tour in Australia last winter ...' Frank Woolley in his autobiography *King of Games*, that came out for the 1936 season, offered a 16 for Australia' as chosen after the 1935 season. It included Sellers under Gubby Allen as captain. Allen, one of the few amateurs able to play for England on merit, lost the Test series in Australia in 1936/37 but, all agreed, did well as captain on and off the field. He could not give enough time to cricket to carry on. Robins, the regular Middlesex captain who could play for England on merit as an all-rounder, was the leading candidate for the 1937 season, ahead of Sellers. 'If only Brian Sellers had been a slightly better bat he would have been the perfect choice as a skipper of many an England touring side,' wrote Yardley later. In other words, Sellers' 'strong personality' would knit together a party abroad for months, a skill not as needed in the English summer. The typically generous Robertson-Glasgow said much the same in his 1941 sketch; Sellers' personal ability 'at its best, has been little below England standard'. In a 1948 book Bill Edrich went further: 'Brian Sellers was so good a skipper that it was a perpetual amazement to all cricketers that he was never selected to lead England.' Could Sellers make up for a lack of runs from his bat by saving runs with his field placings, taking wickets thanks to his bowling changes, and motivating others? To do for England what he did for Yorkshire? It was plausible enough for those in authority to give him an audition.

On 7 July 1937, the newspapers named Sellers as captain of the Gentlemen against the Players at Lord's, starting a week later. *The Times* approved: 'The North of England wanted him to be given recognition, and at last he has obtained it.' Robins, who had already captained England in the first Test against New Zealand, was not playing. 'Better late than never!' wrote Looker-on in the *Sheffield Telegraph* on the Saturday before the match. He talked up Sellers and looked a year ahead to the next Australian visit:

Brian Sellers is the best captain in the country ... He knows all the 'tricks of the trade'. He is a brilliant fieldsman and extremely popular. He has a happy personality which enables him to get the best out of his men. Sellers has Yorkshire grit: he is a fighter: and against the Australians we shall want a fighter. Much may depend on how he succeeds in next week's representative match.

Bob Wyatt and Norman Mitchell-Innes walked out in the sunshine to open for the Gentlemen. 'There never was a better morning for cricket,' wrote

Howard Marshall in the *Daily Telegraph*. It was the last summer when you could believe, however foolishly, that all was well with the world politically. The Gentlemen were all out for 165 by 3.05 pm for what Marshall called a 'very indifferent' 165. Sellers, who went in at 160 for seven, was hardly to blame for the batsmen above him. Seam bowlers, including the Players captain Wally Hammond, had taken the earlier wickets. Hammond had brought on the Gloucestershire spinner Tom Goddard, presumably knowing tail-enders, and Sellers in particular, would struggle. Sellers duly did. 'Sellers had an over from Goddard when the ball was apparently completely invisible,' Marshall wrote, and escaped stumping by Les Ames three times. Cardus in the *Manchester Guardian* was cruellest to Sellers, who:

lunged forward and missed aim time after time. Once he promised to fall on his chin, and was still reeling when Ames was returning the ball to Goddard. The wonder is that he did not take guard next ball facing Ames. He was stumped at last off Goddard amid general merriment.

It gave Cardus a chance – and he took it – to play the same old gramophone record that batting wasn't what it used to be. Worse for Sellers' prospects, fielding for the Players besides Hammond had been Hutton, Joe Hardstaff and Denis Compton, the sort of younger men he would have to win over as captain. Sellers had shown himself up, and the sour-minded such as Cardus, and all those who disliked Yorkshire, had gloated.

When the Players replied, Sellers was not used to his bowlers; as Cardus noted, 'he himself occupied a post farther from the wicket probably than he has ever visited before'. This had symbolic and practical meaning; Sellers was not central to the play, and he felt unable to set his usual aggressively close fields. The Players were all out on the second morning with a lead of 64. Sellers, again batting at nine, went in when the Gentlemen were only 52 ahead. From the pavilion end Goddard was again flighting his off-breaks cleverly, and the one that went with his arm, and Sellers was still guessing. 'Despite his anxieties, Sellers stayed there however, and was loudly cheered when he pulled Hammond for four, after 25 minutes, his first scoring stroke,' Marshall reported. Sellers and Freddie Brown put on 63 until Brown was caught in the deep for 47. Sellers was left on 20 not out, and left the Players 121 to win, which they knocked off by 6.30 pm. Hutton, Sellers and fellow Gentleman Yardley at least had a free day before they joined Yorkshire at Nottingham on the Saturday. Brown and Goddard were among the England 12 for the next Test. Robins, still captain, was 'the obvious choice', wrote Harold Marshall. Sellers had not passed his audition.

Sellers could only play as an amateur longer than most because he could afford to. When Sellers announced his wedding at the end of the 1932 season, at least one newspaper picked up that it was not yet known if Sellers' 'business duties' would allow him to lead Yorkshire in 1933. According to his son Andrew, Sellers' father Arthur told him 'to get something to do during the winter'. Sellers' father-in-law was an accountant for a business coming up for sale:

Everyone's an expert: A Yorkshire Evening Post cartoon, August 1938, on the England Test selectors.

a small sporting printer in Bradford, and they thought that might be ideal for him, because of his sporting contacts and he said yes, it was a good idea, but he would not go in unless he had his brother who was an accountant with him, because my father didn't have a great sense of money.

Godfrey, also an accountant, ran The Yorkdale Press in the summer, 'and it seemed to work quite well in that respect', Andrew said. Indeed he and his brother David went into the business: 'I think the three-day week [in the 1970s] killed it off.' The Yorkshire finance committee minutes show regular payments to the firm for 'general printing'. While the club did use other printers, a detail from August 1935 suggests that it showed favouritism towards Sellers' company. The committee recommended accepting another firm's quotation of £450 for printing the 1936 yearbook and membership tickets, only for the general committee to ask finance to think again. It duly picked Yorkdale, although its quote totalled £472. If anyone was at fault, it was the club for giving the work, not Yorkdale for taking it. Altogether more dubious was another captain, Ronnie Burnet; the finance committee made him resign in 1968 for holding on to money from sales of Jimmy Binks' and Raymond Illingworth's benefit ties.

Was it unfair to give any man only one chance to prove himself? Did Sellers lack that indefinable 'big match temperament'; or did he fall short of the minimum of ability you needed to make a Test eleven? It must have added to the excitement before another big match eight weeks later; between the champions Yorkshire and the challengers Middlesex. Robins made the challenge by telegram in late August. Sellers wired back to accept, offering stakes of £10 per man and asked Robins to choose the ground. It might sound harmless enough today, and certainly it 'caught the public fancy', as *Country Life* magazine wrote, as an end to 'a season of gay and

*Yorkdale Press staff at retirement presentation for composing room foreman Harry Woodhead, May 1975. Brian Sellers, still with his hair parted down the middle, is in white to the right of the table. His brother Godfrey is at the back behind the man with spectacles; his son David wearing a tie is behind his left shoulder, as is printer Steve Troth, supplier of this picture. Andrew Sellers is also at the back behind the right-hand woman wearing spectacles.
Others from left are Herbert ? – linotype operator and compositor; Arnold ? – compositor; unknown; Ted ? – handyman-driver; unknown, unknown; Pat ? – receptionist; Marjorie ? – bench hand finisher; Maggie ? – bench hand finisher; Abdul ? – printer; John ? – guillotine operator; unknown; John Gledhill – printer; sitting at the table are Mr and Mrs Woodhead; Vinnie Towers – printer; Bob Shutt – compositor; unknown; and Charlie Broadbent – machine room foreman.*

gallant cricket'. Ever the more practical, the *Yorkshire Post* pointed out that Middlesex had run Yorkshire close and rain had spoiled their match at Sheffield. Sellers said: 'It should do the game a power of good. It should be a grand match.' Some disapproved, including Lord Hawke, living in retirement at North Berwick. Quite apart from the novelty, instead of a match between the champions and the rest, and captains showing minds of their own, some worried about commercialism or corruption. *Country Life* had thrilled to the 'ancient and romantic days of cricket', when men threw down challenges. However, as the magazine admitted, wagers could mean betting, which was 'ungallant and sordid'. Once Yorkshire had indeed won the Championship at the end of August, the Yorkshire committee met to agree. Hawke still grumbled, but said he did not want to take a 'dog in the manger attitude'. It was a watershed; Sellers, his father and the club, had defied Hawke; and a year later, Hawke was dead.

Yorkshire did to Middlesex what they did to so many teams when Sellers won the toss. On the first, cold day Yorkshire made 293 for five. On the Monday they closed on 401 and Middlesex slid to 63 for six. According to Cardus, the not out batsman Owen-Smith appealed about the bad light to Sellers, 'who came to the wicket, looked down it into the cavern of the pavilion, and then reluctantly ordered his men to cease fire'. In Middlesex's second innings, the 48-year-old Patsy Hendren was batting for the last time for Middlesex after a 30-year career. Sellers shook his hand and led his team in three cheers. Middlesex lost by an innings inside three days of a four-day match. 'I doubt if anybody will challenge Yorkshire again,' wrote Cardus. Not all were so crabby; many of the crowd gathered outside the pavilion to cheer Yorkshire and called for the captain.

Hammond in 1938 turned amateur and became England captain. Sellers became a selector, as the northerner on the committee. Sellers had already played a part of sorts in England selection on Saturday 13 July 1935. The story is well known; Leyland had a bad back before the Third Test against South Africa at Leeds. Sellers drove to Arthur Mitchell's home in Baildon, a dozen miles away. Mitchell was in his garden, about to enjoy some rest; by 1 pm he was batting for England. Less known is the primitive – by more connected 21st century standards – way the authorities tried to find Mitchell. A blackboard carried around Headingley asked Arthur Mitchell of Yorkshire to go to the pavilion.

In old age Sellers recalled:

Today I think fame comes too quickly – and so does rejection. Take Bill Edrich before the war ... we knew he had the ability and we had to have patience for our judgement. No player would have got the chance today that he got. But we knew he was world class. Well he had a bloody awful series against Australia [in 1938] *and we sent him to South Africa and he had a bloody awful tour until the last game when he got 200 and some, in the last, the timeless Test – the last one* [overseas] *before war broke out.*

A 1930s cartoon of Brian Sellers; truly a larger than life figure?!

Chapter Seven
Wartime

'Tis to die like a beast for a man to leave no memory behind.
Blaise de Montluc, The Habsburg-Valois War
and the French Wars of Religion

In old age Sellers said:

*Herbert Sutcliffe was certainly the greatest batsman I saw, yet but for the war what might have happened for Len [**Hutton**] and Compton and Edrich and Washbrook – six years lost to batsmen who would have been in their prime in that time.*

It would be thoughtless to feel sorry for sportsmen not able to show their talent for a few years, while millions were homeless, bereaved and killed; and as someone who went through the war, Sellers was not crass enough to press the point. Kilburn wrote of Yorkshire that 'a great cricket team broke up' in September 1939. True; except many families, and communities, broke up thanks to that war. Within cricket, the Second World War, like 1914-18, was more than a break to the county round; conscription, evacuation and shortages of goods prevented schools' matches, coaching in the Headingley 'shed', even fathers playing with sons in back gardens and schoolmates playing in yards. In total wars like those if 1914-18 and 1939-45, to attempt to live as in peacetime might be an aid to the enemy. While every county suffered, Yorkshire, further from the Nazi-held Continent, was freer to play cricket than some counties.

In truth the Yorkshire eleven as led by Sellers was due to break up anyway, merely because of age. Of the 13 men that played in one of the last two matches of 1939, only two, Hutton and Yardley, were under 28. In an era when all sorts of county cricketers, not only slow bowlers, could hope to hold their place until 40, about half the team, including Sellers, had years left in them; not so the wicket-keeper Wood, 41; and the batsmen Barber, 38; Mitchell and Turner, 37; Leyland, 39; and Sutcliffe, 44. As Leyland played one last season in 1946, then retired, we can speculate that he might have gone sooner, but for the war. In other words, the war may in fact have postponed the break-up of the team Sellers found himself with in 1946. Even an ideal side like Sellers' has to keep renewing itself; the very success of an ageing team may cause worse decline later if it does not take in younger men in good time. The war interrupted that balance. It meant Yorkshire could not test the next generation, men such as Wardle and Jim Laker; nor bring on those that had reached the first team by 1939, such as Willie Watson. The balance had two sides; the older players passed on

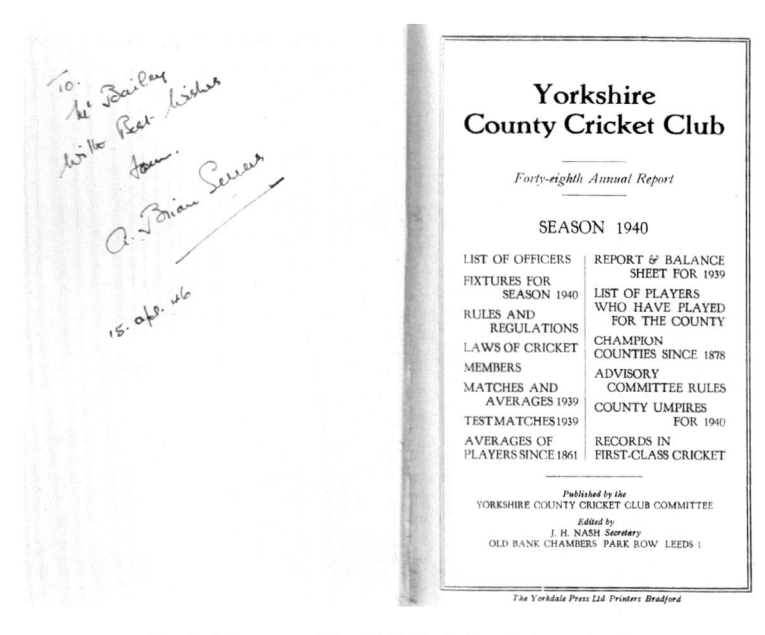

The inside cover of the 1940 Yorkshire club yearbook, signed by Brian Sellers for Allan Bailey (courtesy of Michael Ellison).

their experience to the apprentices. When the County Championship began again in 1946 Sellers or any older man could only try to catch up with the lost schooling of the previous six summers. And one of the masters was not there any more.

In *The Cricketer* in 1968 the Yorkshire journalist John Bapty recalled:

In 1946 ... Hedley's name often turned up in the talk as we travelled about the country ... I remember Sellers on a trip from Canterbury to London speculating on the part there might have been for Verity (38 a couple of months before he was fatally wounded) in Yorkshire's rebuilding and it can be said here and now that Yorkshire's post-war story would have been a very different one had there been no early morning attack in Sicily by the First Battalion The Green Howards on the morning of July 9, 1943.

When news of Verity's death reached England in September 1943, Sellers said in tribute: 'I can only say that I was much honoured to play alongside such a great cricketer and fine character.' Sellers spoke as spectators stood at Bradford before Yorkshire and Lancashire played the memorial match to Verity in aid of his widow and children in August 1945. Can we explain at least some of the widespread and lasting grief over the loss of Verity to the nagging guilt among his fellow players and civilians generally that they had survived, while he had not? Many cricketers, and sportsmen more generally, like many others – actors, writers, dentists - had taken the chance to avoid the front line, by in effect staying in their peacetime occupations.

The front line was a place for young men; yet Verity was a couple of years older than Sellers. Just as Sellers, 32 at the outbreak of war, stood about halfway on the sportsmen's spectrum of how much the war interrupted his playing career, so he stood about halfway on the spectrum of how useful his war duty was. Sellers was neither one of the few genuinely on the front line (Bill Edrich) nor one of the most outrageous shirkers (such as Cardus). As early as October 1939, Sellers, Smailes and Leyland were in photographs in newspapers as gunners in an anti-aircraft unit. That early in the war, fears of bombing were genuine, and such service was worthy. As newspapers were recalling as late as Verity's death, under Sellers the Yorkshire team set an example by joining the forces at the opening of the war, when – it's easy to forget now – the country flinched from another war. If Sellers faced any moral test - grotesque and pointless though it is for us to ask – he passed it then.

Joining an anti-aircraft unit in 1939:
Maurice Leyland, Frank Smailes, unknown, Brian Sellers.

Nor was Sellers doing anything different from his wider peers; when he captained an Anti-Aircraft Command team at Lord's in May 1943 that beat a team from Balloon Command (that is, static anti-aircraft balloons), among the 22 were his colleague Cyril Turner and such county players as T.N.Pearce, M.D.Lyon, Jack Parker and Alec Bedser. Such posts did prove less dangerous than the life of an infantryman, pilot or seaman.

Just as returned soldiers from any war find that civilians do not want to know about their battles, let alone thank them, so Sellers and others did not get credit for their peacetime achievements that peaked on the eve of war. *Wisden's Almanack* for 1940 made Sellers one of their five cricketers of the year – that is, 1939 – alongside Constantine, Bill Edrich, Keeton and Doug Wright. Nothing was normal any more – that year's edition did not come out until June – and as Robertson-Glasgow noted inside, to look back at 1939 was already 'like peeping curiously through the wrong end of a telescope'. Hence whatever *Wisden*'s verdict on Sellers – and the sketch naming him as one of the five hailed him as 'the most successful county captain of all time' – the fall of France and the Battle of Britain overshadowed it. The article also quoted Sellers' opinion 'that a clever bowler with ten good fieldsmen can shut out the game except when such batsmen as Bradman, Woolley, Leyland or Hammond take command. His contention is that such a bowler rather than the watchful batsman causes slow cricket.' This made sense on that profound point of how to keep cricket watchable in an ever more demanding leisure market with ever more alternatives; however, the summer of 1940 was hardly the time for anything about cricket to stick in the public mind.

Just as politicians well before the end of the war could debate the country after the war, so the MCC set up a 'select committee' under the distinguished former Yorkshire amateur Sir Stanley Jackson, to report on county cricket. It met on a Tuesday in December 1943 and January 1944 and reported in mid-March. Sellers was only one of eight amateurs and captains on the committee; the others were Hammond, the Nottinghamshire captain George Heane, A.J.Holmes of Sussex, E.R.T.Holmes of Surrey, Robins, Maurice Turnbull (to die in France in August) and Bob Wyatt. With so much in common, they were hardly going to disagree, nor demand drastic change; least of all Sellers, having done so well in the 1930s. It is however striking that – in contrast with parliamentary politics of the time, that saw such legislation as the 1944 Education Act – the MCC committee set itself against change. The committee saw nothing wrong with county cricket's shape or style. It ended one 1939 experiment, of the eight-ball over, and proposed another, a new ball after 55 overs. It was against play on Sunday 'for obvious reasons', so obvious it didn't say what – presumably, the law; it stood by matches of two innings, without time or overs limits on an innings, to give 'the fullest scope for skilled captaincy to reap its reward'. It did suggest a knock-out competition, but of matches over three days. It was against merging any counties; or dividing the championship into two, 'as this would appear to spell financial disaster for those in the lower half of the table'. It urged the county game to resume as soon as it could after the war, and suggested four 'emergency' regions: north, Midlands, south west and south east. In the event, the end of the war against Germany and then Japan in 1945 gave enough time to begin as normal in 1946. While you can never see the hand of anyone in such bland outcomes – indeed, committees pride themselves on being unanimous – it does show how Sellers, the 'crackerjack' captain, was fully in line with the conservatives in authority at Lord's; whether in such empty slogans as 'the players shall adopt a dynamic attitude towards the game' or the more meaningful 'the team shall aim for victory from the first ball and maintain an enterprising attitude until the last over'. That could have been Sellers' motto. As an editorial in the *Times* summed up approvingly, the committee wanted to restore county cricket, as 'more of a game and less of an organized business'. The champion county, whose challenge match in 1937 had been in aid of charities, was bound to agree.

*Brian Sellers' MBE for wartime service,
in the possession of his daughter-in-law Anne Sellers.*

Lord's might not want the game to change; but it could hardly order everyone to go back to the people they were in 1939. Experiences changed men; and even if some men did not change, other men, that were changed, would affect them. In his 1997 book *Talking Cricket*, Fred Trueman told a wartime story – a sign of how long they can go the rounds – of the Nottinghamshire batsman Charlie Harris, who played at Lord's for an Army team captained by Sellers. Because Sellers told his men to be smart and correct, Harris mischievously came to attention and marched to his fielding position each over. He was risking a confrontation with Sellers by clowning; but like all clowns, Harris was pointing out a truth; the similarity in discipline between a sports team and a military unit. Whether a man took to uniformed life might depend on how similar it was to his life before. There are few records of Sellers' years in the Army, whether because he did little or because it was the done thing not to make anything of your service, in case it looked like boasting. Sellers did play for, and arrange and captain, teams that played around the country, in aid of charity, often in front of large crowds. The men, usually in services teams, were mixed, as presumably was the quality of the one-day matches. We cannot read much into any batting or bowling, such as Sellers' 114 at Epsom in June 1943 in a 12-a-side match between Monty Garland-Wells' team and locals, though each side had several current or future county players. The cricketers were keeping their eye in, and their matches served to keep cricket flickering, like a candle after a power cut. More ominous was that by 1944 Sellers had become a major, one rank above a captain in the Army. After years of telling men in uniform what to do, on returning to Yorkshire in charge of men in whites, without older men over him such as Lord Hawke and his father, Sellers would have ever fewer brakes on him in the county club. He would have only himself to rely on that his leadership did not become tyranny, and that his judgement was sound.

Interlude
Team photographs

Although images drench our age, we do not read images as much as we might. Compare these two Yorkshire team photographs.

As the one with Brian Sellers has a young Len Hutton, it must date from around 1935. The captain sat, as was typical, at the centre. The senior pro Herbert Sutcliffe was his right-hand man; and the support staff, Ringrose the scorer and Heyhirst the masseur, stood on the margins. Perhaps expressions and stances give clues into individual character; or perhaps we read into them what we think we know. Hutton as the youngest looks least at ease; Leyland, 'pleasant and easy-going' as Bowes described him. Was Bowes, holding his left wrist with his right hand, feeling for his pulse? Or bashful? We can try to read the ensemble too. Each of the men wore a blazer, buttoned up. Every man had his own space, no more or less. Whether the pose was by design or natural, these men look a well-drilled group.

Back row (l to r): Ringrose, Robinson, Verity, Smailes, Turner, Hutton, Heyhirst. Seated; Barber, Bowes, Sutcliffe, Sellers, Leyland, Mitchell, Wood.

Interlude – Team photographs

What a contrast with Geoffrey Wilson, the captain from 1922 to 1924, and his team! Norman Kilner on the left and Maurice Leyland on the right were not wearing their blazer. Wilfred Rhodes (by then the greatly experienced all-rounder and the captain's symbolic and presumably actual right-hand man) had his unbuttoned. These men were not uniform; in this team men could be different, or resisted uniformity – and authority? Who said so: the captain, or the players? The men were spread unevenly – Leyland as one of the youngest and most junior players, and the scorer on the right had most room, on the symbolic edge of the scene, while several men were wedged around their skipper. If you put your hand over the list of names and ignored the county caps, you might think that the man seated in the middle was a captive.

Geoffrey Wilson, formerly of Harrow School and Cambridge University, the only man wearing a muffler, was very much the odd man out. Note particularly the taut arms of George Macaulay, resting on the bench behind Wilson. Was that a sign of Macaulay – though a junior bowler then – asserting himself? Note also Wilson's defensively folded arms, while Arthur Dolphin and Percy Holmes had theirs more confidently open. Dolphin and Rhodes, not their captain, rested their shoulders against the wooden bench as if they owned it. Wilson was a Yorkshire captain with little room of his own. The images speak of how a workplace's culture can change in a dozen years, and the difference that a man with force of character can make.

Standing (l to r): Edgar Oldroyd, Norman Kilner, Roy Kilner, Herbert Sutcliffe, George Macaulay, Abe Waddington, Maurice Leyland, H Nottingham (scorer). Seated: Emmott Robinson, Wilfred Rhodes, Geoffrey Wilson (captain), Arthur Dolphin, Percy Holmes.

Interlude – Team photographs

As for the later 1930s team, which has one difference – Norman Yardley has joined, to take a central place between Sellers and Leyland – note the slight space between Sellers' and Yardley's arms. Which of the two men has made that gap? Does it speak of an emotional distance, a wariness by the captain towards the man already likely to take over from him? Or was Sellers giving Yardley space to grow?

Back row (l to r): Bright Heyhirst (masseur), Cyril Turner, Ellis Robinson, Hedley Verity, Bill Bowes, Len Hutton, Frank Smailes, William Ringrose (scorer). Seated: Arthur Mitchell, Arthur Wood, Herbert Sutcliffe, Brian Sellers, Norman Yardley, Maurice Leyland, Wilf Barber.

Chapter Eight
Treachery in Australia 1946/47

For what is treachery? It is the betrayal of familiars to strangers ...
Rebecca West, The Meaning of Treason (1949)

If Sellers and his fellow passengers didn't feel it on Sunday 13 October 1946, as they walked along the wooden jetty to the motor boat that would take them to their flying boat in Poole harbour, they did feel it the following Saturday morning when they stepped off it onto another boat at Rose Bay, and saw the Sydney Harbour Bridge. They had done more than cross the British Empire - stopping overnight in Rangoon and Singapore - on a thrilling, glamorous and expensive 12,400 miles journey, barely imaginable until well into Sellers' lifetime. They had left the early winter of England for the early summer of Australia; left a country literally and perhaps metaphorically exhausted for a sunny one.

Sellers had agreed to cover the MCC's tour of Australia for the *Yorkshire Evening Post* - after the rival *Yorkshire Evening News* hired Bill Bowes - in August. Sellers had ended the 1946 season at Scarborough in good batting form; he was top scorer for Yorkshire when they followed on against MCC, and drew; and for the North in their first innings when they beat the South. The MCC tourists and reporters were already sailing for Australia.

Sellers like so many felt the pull of Australia: English-speaking, yet attractively unlike England; an outdoors culture, a land of plenty. In November he told readers of 'a small snack' with coffee: 'tomato soup, large fillet steak, two fried eggs, onions, chips, pot of tea and as much bread and butter as I could eat, all for three shillings'. He knew such detail would leave readers envious, starting their eighth winter on rations. 'Everyone here is most kind. They feel they can't do enough for you and are always asking you about England. I will refrain from mentioning again anything about food.' A cousin in Sydney that Sellers hadn't seen for 17 years had taken him in hand on arrival. After four days of 'lovely surf beaches' and other sights, he was in 'lovely' Melbourne for the Melbourne Cup - 'the whole town seems to close down for this day' - and with other journalists travelled by bus for 15 hours to 'beautiful' Adelaide. By Friday 25 October he was reporting on the men he and other selectors had picked. They had docked in Western Australia a couple of weeks before he set off, and were now making 506 for five declared against Bradman's South Australia. 'I can see that I am in for a wonderful trip among charming people,' he wrote. What could go wrong?

On 15 October, while Sellers was on the BOAC flying boat - probably over

*The MCC selectors, 1946:
left to right, Walter Robins, Walter Hammond, AJ Holmes and Brian Sellers.*

India – the *Evening Post* printed Sellers' first article, on the prospects for the tour. Naturally, as one of the selectors, he talked up their chances. He saw 'stacks of runs in the batting', including 'of course the master, the great Hammond'. As for the bowling, Alec Bedser was 'in for a lot of hard work' and Doug Wright was the likely spearhead; otherwise, it proved pitifully, and predictably, weak. Even before the event, Sellers was excusing the choices: Bill Voce, who had turned 37 ('true, we haven't seen a lot of him since the war'), the 40-year-old James Langridge and 34-year-old Dick Pollard ('stock bowlers') and the little-bowled Jack Ikin ('may bowl better than some think possible'). While, as he admitted, 'a fairly old team' – the median age was 32 - it did have 'a vast amount of experience' and yet many new to Australia. In fairness, as MCC had not toured there for ten years, thanks to war, the selectors could not help that. For the first time the tourists had a masseur: 'a small but in my view after my experience with Yorkshire an important point'. They had 'every chance to win', Sellers said, and the bowlers 'might cause a surprise'; and in any case winning was 'not of paramount importance'. Like the Australian Services team in the Victory summer of 1945, this tour was to encourage cricket. That sounded odd, coming from Sellers. They were about to find out that Australia needed no encouraging.

Also odd, and something the *Post* made much of, was Sellers' conflict of interest. He was giving his 'expert estimate' as the man who selected the 17. When the newspaper got its man, it called him 'our Test writer'; naturally, because it wanted its money's worth. Yet how could he criticise the men he had chosen? If he only said kind things, would he be a proper reporter? A man cannot serve two masters; which is probably why so few selectors have been reporters. In reply to the MCC's 506 for five, Bradman made 76; 'batting practice with an eye on the future', Sellers called it. Because Bradman had injured his groin slightly while fielding, 'the quick singles for which he is famous were not taken but even with one leg he would score more runs than I ever would!' Sellers was honest about himself and generous towards others; Bradman was still 'a very great player and I only hope he will play in the Tests'. Sellers was already offering his philosophy – Edrich, though quick, was bowling too many balls off the wicket, 'just a waste of energy, that's all'. Sellers, watching through binoculars, knew what to look for. After the vice-captain Yardley led MCC to a win over Victoria in Melbourne, Sellers praised him, 'though I thought he would have done better after lunch to have brought third man to slip'. Yardley had changed his bowlers well but left gaps in the field, 'and he must study the batsmen a bit more'. Sellers already saw faults ('the bowling will improve with better fielding'). Still at Melbourne, a thunderstorm and hailstones as big as peas, 'to make me feel quite homesick' meant no play on the first day against an Australian XI. Sellers noted that Hutton in the field slowed as he neared the ball, after he had slipped once: 'in this game you must be well spiked or else you cannot do your stuff'. Yardley and Hutton played under Sellers at Yorkshire and would have to take the criticism; but could others, above all Hammond, the captain and the greatest English cricketer of his time?

On 12 November, with the first Test in Brisbane 17 days away, Sellers sounded more strident: 'One thing stands out a mile and that is that the fielding is not up to standard by a very long way. If there is no improvement before long we shan't win the Test and that is a certainty.' A week later, he reported that the Australian 12 was younger than England's, 'which will give them an advantage in the field'. Hadn't the selectors thought of how the huge, hot ovals of Australia called for young legs? As Sellers had never been to Australia before, perhaps not.

England captain Wally Hammond.

By Friday 22 November, a week before the Test, Sellers and the touring party were in Brisbane. The next day Sellers made the *Post*'s front page: 'Brian Sellers criticises Hammond'. The newspaper called it 'pointed criticism'; only by 1946, rather than 21st century standards. Sellers stuck to examples and avoided abuse. He wrote as one captain about another. Hammond's captaincy had surprised him 'a great deal. His field placings I cannot understand'. Sellers wished to see Hammond 'smile a bit more and give some encouragement to the team when they do anything'. This incidentally gave insight into how Sellers led men: 'A word now and then does wonders.' At times Sellers sounded more like the anxious selector: 'Ikin has hardly bowled at all. Hutton not at all. Why he didn't use non-regular bowlers more is beyond me ... when things aren't going right the skipper must experiment with non-regulars.' And Sellers returned to the fielding; which had improved, 'but more attention must be paid to backing up. Many runs have been thrown away through not doing this.'

Sellers had said some of it in the weeks before. He caused a sensation now, in the English and Australian press, for two reasons. One was timing, which is one of the ingredients of news. The nearer to the First Test, the more any comment mattered. Whether Sellers had a point or not, any warning by any Englishman, especially from one so 'expert', became a news story, before the actual cricket.

Why did Sellers say it? By accepting the job, he had risked the charge of hypocrisy. That had not stopped the *Post* offering the job – naturally, because controversy sold newspapers. Had the prospect of a winter in Australia, and a seat at the much-anticipated Tests, turned Sellers' head? Was he like Bill Bowes trying the life of a correspondent for size?

To put the question another way; could the selectors have chosen another captain? Sellers, Robins and chairman of selectors A.J.Holmes, appointed in April 1946, had chosen Hammond for the Tests against the touring Indians. When Hammond captained England in June 1946 at Lord's against the Rest, the other captain was Bryan Valentine. If Hammond had given up or been injured, other men were around; they always are. As Hammond was batting as well as ever, it would have taken brave selectors to overlook Hammond, and the veterans, the known and the obvious. To pick the tour party, three aged Lord's grandees – Sir Stanley Jackson, Sir Pelham Warner and Lord Cobham – joined the selectors. They were plainly there to make sure the choices were unobjectionable to the sort of men they met in gentlemen's clubs and even the House of Lords. As in cabinet government, one member may disagree with the majority, but he either has to accept the decisions or resign. Sellers, like any selector, owed loyalty. Cliff Cary, a journalist covering the tour, was convinced afterwards 'that had Sellers possessed the power to alter the touring party, there would have been many radical changes long before the First Test'. Cary felt Sellers criticised Hammond, 'so caustically' to wake him up. Except: couldn't Sellers have avoided the embarrassment of finding fault with the captain, who he helped to choose, by telling him in private?

More to the point, did it work? Journalists asked Hammond to reply. He did, rather stiltedly: 'Mr Sellers is on the same basis as any other journalist with the MCC party and is entitled to write as he pleases. No strained relations exist between us.' The mass-market *Daily Express* on 27 November - always ready to keep stirring a pot - suggested the opposite; that there were 'strained relations'. It reported that Sellers 'was at one time discussed as a possible member of the touring team'; in other words, insinuating that Sellers might have wanted Hammond's job. The next day the *Express* and others did report Sellers laughing and joking with Hammond and wishing him the best of luck. Even if it was genuine, couldn't Hammond have done without the bother, on the eve of the first Test against Australia for eight years? In a 1959 memoir Bill Edrich, one of the 1946 tourists, wrote: 'Cut Hammond and he bled like any other human being. And that is what happened here. He was deeply hurt and the morale of the team around him dropped.' Edrich was one of the few to speak in terms of feelings; and even he implied that Sellers wrote what he did for

Hammond and his first wife Dorothy Lister, at their wedding at Bingley parish church, with bat and wickets for the press cameras (presumably?).

Crowds outside the Hammonds' wedding in Bingley in April 1929.

cricketing reasons. Except that Sellers might have had private reasons to take on Hammond, who had married in 1929, at Bingley parish church, a Bingley lady, Dorothy Lister, daughter of a Bradford wool merchant. In the small world of West Riding business families, did Sellers (or his wife) know her, and resent that Hammond was divorcing her for another woman?

Sellers did not stop criticising Hammond. During the Third Test, when a big Australian eighth-wicket stand took the match and thus the series away from England, Sellers wrote: 'Hammond still had two slips and a gully and no man out. I cannot say why but there it was for everyone to see.' That said, Sellers gave due praise. Three weeks later when Hammond's 188 against South Australia included his 50,000[th] first-class run, Sellers reported: 'Everyone was delighted to see Hammond's return to form.' And a month after, before Hammond's bad back kept him out of the final Test, Sellers hoped he would be fit to play: 'I feel sure he must get some runs some time. He cannot go on missing all the way.'

Sellers stayed out of another controversy, over leg before decisions by the home umpires against English batsmen. His was the voice of the cricketer who accepted that umpires made mistakes like everyone else, and some would go for you, some against: 'All sorts of things happen in cricket. That is what makes it worthwhile playing.' He criticised English batsmen for not going down the wicket to spinners, and (repeatedly) told Doug Wright to bowl slower and give the ball more air. Unlike some journalists, who never admitted they were ever wrong, but who expected everyone on the field to be perfect, Sellers was frank about his shortcomings. When Wright bowled Bradman for 12 in the last Test, Sellers commented: 'It was a bad shot – the sort of shot I play and one does not expect Bradman to do that sort of thing so early in his innings.' Sellers, then, was rather a good correspondent. His son Andrew, 70 years on, said that reporting was 'not really his forte, I would have thought; anyway he had a go at it, and he seemed to enjoy the trip a lot, very much so'. Informed and observant, Sellers gave criticism or credit when it was deserved and could show sympathy and wit. When Yardley bowled Bradman in the third Test, Sellers joked, 'we shall have to call him the atom splitter'.

Few brought up the November controversy afterwards; but they could still remember, and hold it against him. Sir Stanley Jackson at the time spoke of an 'understanding' that selectors would not write about players they picked until the end of a season; if so, Sellers evidently did not understand. Otherwise the MCC played the usual dead bat. The club secretary Lieutenant Colonel R.S.Rait Kerr said he had not seen the article and in any case would not comment: 'Mr Sellers is in Australia purely as the correspondent of a newspaper and not in any capacity as a representative of the MCC.' Could you take off responsibility and loyalty like a hat? Even in Hammond's county, the *Bristol Evening World* thought you could. The newspaper had sounded sorrowful rather than angry: 'it hardly seems cricket to launch such an attack'. Yardley in his memoir called the criticism 'outspoken' and recalled it 'caused some dismay'. That might help us analyse the invitation to Sellers from the touring players to join their Saturday night club, 'at which they and a few privileged friends throw off the cares of big cricket for a couple of hours'. The invite only came in January; had the players waited to see what else Sellers printed? Sellers like others praised Godfrey Evans' wicket-keeping. Evans had already played under Sellers in wartime friendlies. In a memoir Evans admitted he did not know Sellers well but described him as 'a man who said what he thought' and a 'great character under whom I should like to have played'. Edrich, however, in a memoir after he had safely retired from Middlesex, called Sellers' criticism 'inexcusable'. Significantly, Edrich objected on the principle: 'I am not saying his opinions were wrong but he had no right to attack his captain while a match or series was in progress.' Sellers' offence was to betray the small, sensitive world of English cricket in public.

According to Kilburn, the resentment puzzled Sellers, who had only said what he believed to be true. Sellers 'undoubtedly suffered some loss of prestige'. Learie Constantine as a West Indian was free to speak his mind. Sellers had 'rather blotted his copybook', he wrote in his 1950 book *Cricket Crackers*: ' ... the whole thing should have been forgotten and Sellers could have captained the 1948 and 1949 Test teams for England. But cricket in England does not work out that way.'

By March 1947, Sellers was no longer an MCC selector. Yardley, as the new England captain, was the committee's northerner instead. Sellers did however become a selector again, in 1949 and 1950; in 1951 Yardley became chairman of selectors; and when Yardley stepped down Sellers returned for the 1955 season.

His son Andrew recalled a story from Sellers' time as a selector, and while he drove a 'Bradford van', by the Bradford motor company Jowett:

I learned to drive on one of those things. He had one for ten years, and he was down in Birmingham, a Test match in Birmingham, and he was staying at the same hotel as, oh crikey now, Freddie Brown, the captain of England at that stage. So father offered to give him a lift to the ground in his van. Which they did and they got to the front gate and of course they were stopped because they didn't have vans in there, there were only Rolls-Royces and Jaguars. In those days it wasn't a wind-down window, it was a pull-down window; 'what seems to be the problem?'. 'You can't come in here without the correct documentation.' He says, 'right, my name is Brian Sellers,'

and he explained that he was a selector, "and if you look across into the passenger side over here, that fellow is called Freddie Brown who is the captain of the bloody team. So he says, 'we either come in or the flaming game doesn't start, one or the other.' And he was waved in quickly; he enjoyed that sort of thing." What spoils the story is that Brown never played a Test match at Birmingham; Andrew Sellers, understandably, like all of us, can be weak on inessential details. Brown did play in a Test trial at Birmingham in 1953. What matters most is that Sellers was there at all; as a true amateur he was happy to put in the time as a selector; the November 1946 episode had not affected his abilities; he was essentially sound. Perhaps the MCC could forgive, despite what Constantine said. Or, more cynically, because Hammond curiously faded out of English cricket, Sellers was free to carry on, despite that blotted copybook; provided he behaved.

Sellers did not repeat the offence. Indeed, ironically, or hypocritically like many in cricket who have taken the media's money, he hated - or at least distrusted - journalists. One of them, Don Mosey, once wrote how Sellers called him 'that shit who writes about Yorkshire cricket'. Mosey told of how the two met at Harrogate after Sellers had been in hospital for a hip operation, because of arthritis:

He spotted me walking through the drizzle towards the pavilion, waved one of the sticks on which he was hobbling, and roared over the heads of the startled (and very wet) spectators, 'I suppose you'll be sorry to see me around again.' 'No,' I replied, 'As one of them-there to another, welcome back.' He took this in, considered it, then bellowed a great laugh. We never had a cross exchange of words after that.

In any chapter of Sellers' life, he ought to have the last word. Tom Graveney in one of his memoirs told the story of Sellers playing at Bristol in May 1947, the first time after the winter's controversy. Hammond had retired. As Sellers walked to the wicket, barrackers shouted: 'Fetch Wally.'

'That's reet,' Sellers called back. 'I'm here. T'other bloke isn't.'

Chapter Nine
Last seasons 1946-48

The few players left from the 1930s soon found that it was not easy for them to make close contact with the new generation of cricketers.
JM Kilburn, Cricket Decade (1959)

He was never short of words, even at Bristol on Tuesday 25 May 1948. Everything went wrong on that final day. It began with Yorkshire 302 ahead with nine wickets standing. Yorkshire wanted quick runs, to then declare; instead they lost seven wickets in the first hour for 43. Sellers batting at nine made 29 not out, and set Gloucestershire 389 in four and a half hours. Watson and Coxon dropped catches off Charles Barnett, who made 141. If catches win matches, dropped catches lose matches. Gloucestershire won by six wickets. George Baker of the *Bristol Evening World* reported: 'I sat a yard away from Yorkshire bowler Bill Bowes in the press box and he made no audible comment.' Sellers had to walk through the 'admiring throng' that welcomed the batsmen and then the fielders to the pavilion – because beating Yorkshire still mattered. A 19-year-old Tom Graveney had been waiting as next man in. Ten years later he recalled that Sellers stood in the doorway of Gloucestershire's dressing room. 'Well played, you lot,' he said. 'But I'll ne'er declare against yer again.' That defiance hid an admission; if Yorkshire's bowling was so weak - without Verity and Bowes, or rather without young bowlers to replace them – and if the captain could no longer set a target, the county could never hope to win enough games to be champions.

Yorkshire would have to build again; and did, under Yardley; the county tied with Middlesex for the Championship in 1949. That Yorkshire came seventh in 1947 and fourth in 1948 in Sellers' last seasons – in 1948 Yardley was captain, and Sellers only stood in when Yardley was leading England against Australia – showed that Sellers could not win with any team. That might seem ammunition for the critics who said that his great side of the 1930s would have won under anyone. If so, how did Yorkshire become champions in 1946, when so many of the 1930s men had gone, or were shadows of themselves? That unusually level 1946 season, when every county was starting anew, showed the difference that Sellers made.

In his 1941 sketch, Robertson-Glasgow had already seen Sellers as 'probably, the one above all others to whom cricketers must look after the war to guide the first-class game along the lines of sense and enjoyment'. In July 1946, just before he made his first-class debut, Johnny Wardle was playing for the Yorkshire first team against Scotland in Glasgow, when Sellers lost the toss and Scotland batted. Sellers kept Yorkshire in the field

Last seasons 1946-48

The 1946 Yorkshire team in soccer kit, at Bradford Park Avenue. The grins of some suggest they saw the humour of being on an unfamiliar field of play; the distance in the centre between Norman Yardley and Len Hutton may speak of tension.

most of the day, despite drizzle: 'Look chaps,' Wardle remembered Sellers saying. 'there is a whole lot of spectators dying to see the Yorkshire side for the first time since before the war and it is up to us to carry on until the crowd goes home or the rain really pours down.' The next month in the Roses match at Manchester, Kilburn in the *Yorkshire Post* estimated 36,500 were inside the ground, making the field of play 'an island of green amid the surging tide of humanity'. Thousands could not get in, and outside 'tried to judge the progress of the game by the applause'. Such was the public appetite for leisure, like a burst dam after war held back the natural flow for years. Sellers responded to it; except the men he used to turn to were not the same. In July 1945, for instance, Sellers led an Army team of all county players against the Royal Australian Air Force in a single innings match. *The Times* called it 'one of the most disappointing games' at Lord's for a long time as the RAAF made 253 and bowled the Army for 70. Bowes, after near three years as a prisoner of war, 'as could be expected, lacked his usual fire', yet Sellers gave him 20 overs. Winning or losing in the 1945 season, the lull after the storm, did not matter so much. While playing for H.D.G.Leveson-Gower's eleven at Scarborough, in the first festival for seven years, after the Australian Services made a remarkable 477 for eight on the first day, Sellers and Coxon, together at 187 for seven, added 53. Sellers hit Jack Pettiford for a six, then was caught off a mis-hit. The championship that mattered would begin again in 1946.

The Times in its preview of the 1946 season summed up: 'It will indeed be a fine performance by any county that finishes above Yorkshire.' Such was Yorkshire's reputation made in living memory. Yet county cricket had never known such a long break. Like commuters in a train strike reminding themselves how to ride a bicycle, whoever got the hang of the old routine first would do best. Only seven of the 17 counties still had their pre-war captains: besides Sellers, T.N.Pearce (Essex), J.C.Clay (Glamorgan), Hammond (Gloucestershire), Robins (Middlesex), George Heane (Nottinghamshire), Bunty Longrigg (Somerset) and Peter Cranmer (Warwickshire). Note that the champions in the first four post-war seasons came from those counties, suggesting teams recovered soonest under an old hand. In their first match at Cambridge, the spinners Arthur Booth, Ellis Robinson and Len Hutton took 14 wickets as Yorkshire crushed the university by an innings. Yorkshire beat Glamorgan at Cardiff, where Robinson and Booth took 16 wickets, then Kent by an innings. Next came Oxford University. The *Oxford Mail* printed a photo of Sellers, having won the toss, taking the field in gauntlets and pads, because wicket-keeper Paul Gibb had a bruised forefinger. The gloves sat unfamiliarly on Sellers, as if he were about to take a casserole out of an oven. As Kilburn put it delicately in the *Yorkshire Post*, Robinson turned the ball enough for Sellers 'to appreciate some of the stresses and distresses of wicket-keeping'. Sellers then top scored with 60, in two and a quarter hours, and with only three fours, while Leyland, batting at eight and limping, made 30 'from what he could reach'. While Yorkshire won easily enough by six wickets, the *Oxford Mail* saw 'little of the aggressiveness normally associated with Yorkshire cricket'. After four wins in four matches, a more hopeful editorial in the *Yorkshire Post* pointed to some fast scoring, sure fielding, a 'bowling attack that is formidable indeed', and a promise by Sellers of 'brighter cricket'. Whether the shortcomings or promises would win out would depend, as ever, at least partly on how good the other counties were.

Rain ruined the first two matches in June, draws against Gloucestershire and Lancashire. Already the pattern for the season was setting: Yorkshire had only Hutton in the country's leading ten batsmen by average, yet three bowlers, Booth, Robinson and Bowes, were among the leading ten bowlers. Yorkshire could keep winning if their batsmen merely made enough runs, and their out-cricket held – and at Lord's for instance when they beat Middlesex in a low-scoring match in mid-June, they took one catch from a ball that bounced off square leg's head. *The Times* praised their 'ruthless determination'. After Yorkshire trailed badly on first innings against Glamorgan at Sheffield, Hutton's 99 not out brought a six-wicket win. Sellers was still setting the standard in the field; the *Sheffield Telegraph* reported how he 'dashed forward from backward point to make a one handed catch almost from the face of Emrys Davies' bat'. Two months into the season, Heyhirst the club masseur was already busy with pulled thigh muscles.

Hutton again top scored in the second innings when Yorkshire won by four wickets at Chesterfield. Hutton made 183 not out as Yorkshire crushed the touring Indians at Bradford by an innings. Six batsmen chipped in for Yorkshire to beat Surrey by six wickets at Headingley. Yorkshire drew with the Indians at Sheffield. Now in mid-July, at about halfway in the

Last seasons 1946-48

Championship, Yorkshire stood second to Lancashire, and the two would tie on points if Yorkshire won their two matches in hand. At halfway on the second day at Taunton Yorkshire were 149 for five in reply to Somerset's 508. Sellers with 50 not out took Yorkshire to 272 for six at the close, and rain saved them on the last day. It showed how Sellers was relying on his leading three bowlers: without Bowes and Booth, Sellers only gave three men, Robinson, Smailes and Coxon, more than 11 overs as it took them 171.4 overs to dismiss Somerset.

Sellers was becoming important with the bat. He and Hutton were the only men in double figures in Yorkshire's first innings at The Oval. The final day began with Yorkshire on 26 for two, needing 112; Surrey let the crowd of a few hundred enter for free (and left out collection boxes). Bruce Harris of the *London Evening Standard* saw the overnight batsmen, the veterans Cyril Turner and Wilf Barber, take all morning and six minutes after lunch to win: 'just as the weariest river winds somewhere safe to sea, so the two Yorkshire indomitables finished at last a voyage in batsmanship,' he wrote. Yorkshire were doing enough, to win. They began August by beating Northamptonshire easily enough by an innings. In that hugely popular match at Old Trafford, Yorkshire began the last day on 42 for two, still needing 174 to make Lancashire bat again. In the previous day's *Yorkshire Post*, Kilburn reviewed the season so far, 'a race between Lancashire and Yorkshire'. Had Kilburn worn spectacles, they would not have been rose-tinted. To suggest the 1946 Yorkshire side compared with many of the past 'would be to invite ridicule' he wrote: 'there is neither the incisiveness in attack nor the overwhelming power in batting of a truly dominating force'. Hutton stood alone as batsman. Fast bowlers were suffering from not enough food. As for the captain:

Sellers himself has several times been guardian of the gate and I should estimate that technically he has never been a better batsman than this season. Paralysis still tends to remain against spin bowling but against the quicker attack and when the ball is lifting uncomfortably his courage and determination have never been in doubt.

That last day bore out Kilburn. Yorkshire batted all day, closing on 220 for five after 125 overs. Sellers and Leyland were unbeaten after a round century stand. Kilburn reported the two men's perfection in their appointed parts, 'character parts of course. Without a mistake or even a real sign of one they played the overs away with their interest all on the pavilion clock and on the scoreboard only in so far as to be assured that numbers five and seven remained against the batsmen.' For winning on first innings Lancashire took four points and Yorkshire none, but Yorkshire denied Lancashire the eight extra points for a win.

Yorkshire could not quite win at Leicester. At Bradford against Warwickshire, rain meant a blank first two days. On a drying pitch Sellers declared on 104 for seven, and took eight points for a single innings win, as Warwickshire were out for 56. If Yorkshire had lost to Lancashire, and not beaten Warwickshire, Lancashire and Yorkshire would have shared the Championship. Yorkshire beat Hampshire at Scarborough where all 40 wickets fell for 418 runs inside two days. Middlesex, the other challengers for the Championship, came to Sheffield. On the first day Sellers won the toss and went into bat at 63 for five. He made 85 not out of the last 163, which Kilburn hailed as 'truly noble': 'He was completely competent in defence and aggression, gave no chance and hit four fours and the crowd of 19,000 rose to cheer at the end of it all.' From 111 for eight, Sellers added 60 with Arthur Booth, who made 29, his career high score. Booth batted one above Bowes but, until his 29, was set, like Bowes, to take more wickets that season than make runs. Even more improbably, Bowes made nine and added 55 with Sellers for the last wicket. Yorkshire took first innings points and began the final day on 82 for two, 139 ahead, seeking quick runs. However after an hour they were 130 for six, and risked defeat. Sellers again made top score of 53, and set Middlesex 260 in three hours. Sellers claimed the last half hour – after losing the first hour of the day to overnight rain – but Yorkshire could only take three of Middlesex's five last wickets.

Fourteen more wickets for Booth and Robinson, and Yorkshire beat Gloucestershire at Headingley; three matches to go. At Eastbourne, Yorkshire trailed Sussex on first innings, 82 to 91. Early on the second day, Monday 26 August, Sussex set Yorkshire 115 to win the match and the Championship. Yorkshire lunched on 34 for four. Sussex scented victory, Kilburn reported. Leyland defended while Frank Smailes attacked and ended on 67 not out, his highest score of the season. Yorkshire won by six wickets. They had become champions for the eighth time in the last ten seasons.

In the *Yorkshire Evening Post*, Little John and Will Watch called the county's 22nd Championship 'the most remarkable of them all when the full account is taken'. The openers had never made a century stand. The batsmen only made six centuries. In a season of much rain and low scoring, Yorkshire were unbeaten. Someone always made a match-saving, or match-winning, innings. Indeed, they wondered in print if Yorkshire might not have been champions if they had made more runs, as they then might have enforced the follow-on, and the unrested bowlers might not have done as well. An editorial in the *Yorkshire Post* praised 'the spirit of the team so perfectly typified in the captain A.B.Sellers'. *The Times* likewise called it a triumph for Sellers, 'who must surely rank among their greatest': 'On and off the field he was a leader, wise and friendly, to a side who responded to a fine example.' In the county's final Championship averages Sellers was third to Hutton and Barber, by number of runs and average.

A ten-wicket defeat by Hampshire at Bournemouth – Sellers top scored in each innings – hardly mattered. Lastly, rain at Trent Bridge prevented a likely innings defeat of Nottinghamshire, after Sellers again top scored. When Yorkshire had to follow on at Scarborough to draw with the MCC, Sellers top scored again.

Newspapers saw it as the end of the great 1930s side. A fortnight earlier, Leyland had said he would retire. Sellers and his deputy Yardley faced a new task; of bringing on several inexperienced players, without many

Last seasons 1946-48

Albert Wilkes & Son, photographers of West Bromwich, took this team picture of Yorkshire at Edgbaston in May 1947. Standing (l to r): Willie Watson, Masseur Heyhirst, Vic Wilson, Alex Coxon, Allan Mason (12th man), Walker (scorer), Harry Crick (wicket-keeper). Seated: Frank Smailes, Bill Bowes, Brian Sellers, Norman Yardley, Len Hutton, Ellis Robinson. Front: Harold Beaumont and Freddie Jakeman (13th man).

other settled older men to share the pastoral work. On his return from Australia in March 1947, Sellers spoke of it as 'a four or five year job'. Little John in the *Evening Post* recalled how Sellers on returning from the war had looked forward to 'perhaps another three years with the side'. 'While he has been in Australia the death of one of his business partners has changed the situation somewhat.'

On the field, 1947 was different too. Yorkshire were weaker, other counties were blooming. No longer would it be, as Bill Edrich said in 1949, looking back, 'an annual race between Yorkshire and the rest'. At Lord's in June 1947 for instance, after two rain-affected days Middlesex were 98 for none in reply to Yorkshire's 187. In two and a half hours Middlesex, the eventual champions, raced to 350 for two declared, looking for an innings win. At 260 for two, when Denis Compton joined Edrich, the *Times* reporter claimed to feel compassion for Yorkshire: 'To see two Yorkshire bowlers of pace bowling with no slip or short-leg, and the fieldsmen spread hopefully around the boundary, was to wonder what transformation had occurred in Yorkshire cricket.' Sellers batted more than an hour for 11, to draw. Yorkshire ended the season joint seventh with Worcestershire, with eight wins, six defeats and 12 draws. That hid an upturn after mid-July, when Yorkshire were twelfth. As the figures suggest, Yorkshire could no longer knock over the likes of Essex. Trevor Bailey in his memoir recalled a draw at Southend in August 1947; Yorkshire made 401 on the first day, only for Essex to make 468 on the second. Sellers had to keep wicket instead of Don Brennan. Ray Smith, batting at ten, took Essex into the lead in a long ninth-wicket partnership.

While standing back to Alex Coxon, the Yorkshire skipper suddenly rose from his rather majestic and somewhat uncomfortable crouch, raised one imperious gloved hand as Alex was about to bowl, walked up to Ray and asked him if he had ever scored a hundred. On being told no, the great man announced to the world in general that he would never have a better bloody chance and then allowed play to continue.

Smith ended on 86 not out.

To return to that 1948 defeat at Bristol after a declaration, as so often the turning point was a missed catch, by Sellers 'of all people' the *Bristol Evening World* reported. When Gloucestershire were 120 for four in their first innings and needed another 43 to save the follow-on, Sellers missed Tom Graveney at mid-wicket; 'a fairly easy chance'. By then Sellers was 41 and had retired the autumn before. While standing in for Yardley in 1948 he still batted usefully; he top scored with 91 as Yorkshire beat the clear leaders and later champions Glamorgan on first innings at Hull; and at Worcester added 106 for the last wicket with Don Brennan. Sellers averaged 34 in the Championship, as if fewer matches and more rest did him good, although the season did favour batsmen. In a hefty 1950 history of Yorkshire in the last 25 years, Kilburn summed up Sellers. He was lucky in taking over a good side; of course he was not always right:

Sometimes the players thought he was carrying determination beyond the point of reason, sometimes his discipline was considered harsh and sometimes he was less than tactful, but his mistakes were those of a man with the strongest sense of duty conscious of carrying a responsibility beyond personal considerations. He neither courted favour nor feared unpopularity and he never shirked a task however distasteful which he regarded as part of the duty of his office.

What that meant for a player emerging after the war, Johnny Wardle spoke of in his memoir. At the cold Headingley nets in April 1947, several players were standing around in overcoats. 'Suddenly there burst forth a roar as from a loud hailer on the bridge of a tramp steamer in a gale.' Sellers suggested the players had better ways to keep warm. 'Johnny,' Wardle thought to himself, 'if he blasts the big boys like that, what is he going to do to the infants department? And that means you.' Wardle revealed that the upturn from mid-July 1947 came after Sellers cleared the Trent Bridge dressing room of everyone except the players and tore into them: 'You have got to concentrate on every single ball all the match and have enough concentration left to keep an eye on me into the bargain,' Sellers said. It's worth listing the ten that had to take the telling-off: in batting order, Hutton, Willie Watson, Yardley, Gerald Smithson, Alec Coxon, Frank Smailes, Wardle, Brennan, Bowes and Booth; in other words, all past, present or future England players except Booth. Sellers was, as Wardle said, 'no respecter of persons'.

Wardle told also how at Harrogate in June 1948, when wet ground delayed play, Sellers marched Wardle around the ground ('Brian never strolls') while giving him 'the dressing down of my life'. The bell rang for play to

Last seasons 1946-48

YORKSHIRE v. MIDDLESEX
(W. E. Bowes' Benefit)
Played at Leeds, 28th, 30th June, and 1st July, 1947
Yorkshire lost by 87 runs at 6.27 p.m. on the second day

MIDDLESEX

First Innings		Second Innings	
S. M. Brown, c Robinson, b Bowes	1	lbw, b Wardle	33
J. D. Robertson, b Coxon	0	lbw, b Wardle	20
W. J. Edrich, b Robinson	70	b Robinson	102
D. C. S. Compton, c Hutton, b Coxon	4	c Coxon, b Wardle	15
R. W. V. Robins, c Bowes, b Coxon	8	b Wardle	0
F. G. Mann, c Sellers, b Bowes	11	c and b Robinson	0
A. Thompson, b Robinson	4	st Brennan, b Wardle	11
L. Compton, c Smailes, b Bowes	21	c Yardley, b Wardle	34
W. F. Price, b Bowes	3	lbw, b Robinson	1
J. A. Young, not out	1	not out	3
L. Gray, c Hutton, b Robinson	0	c Robinson, b Wardle	1
Extras	1	Extras	14
Total	124	Total	234

Runs at the fall of each wicket—

	1	2	3	4	5	6	7	8	9	10
1st Innings	0	2	7	17	36	65	104	114	124	124
2nd Innings	43	64	65	87	87	88	127	218	232	234

YORKSHIRE

First Innings		Second Innings	
L. Hutton, b Edrich	4	c Compton, L., b Young	16
W. Watson, lbw, b Edrich	0	b Edrich	1
H. Halliday, c Price, b Young	11	c Price, b Young	19
N. W. D. Yardley, lbw, b Compton, D.	41	b Young	0
A. B. Sellers, c Robertson, b Compton, D	3	c Robertson, b Compton, D.	31
T. F. Smailes, not out	6	c Edrich, b Young	0
A. Coxon, lbw, b Young	0	c Edrich, b Young	0
J. H. Wardle c Thompson b Compton, D.	0	lbw, b Robins	35
W. E. Bowes, c Robertson, b Young	4	c Compton, L., b Compton, D.	11
D. V. Brennan, b Young	6	not out	12
E. P. Robinson, c Brown, b Compton, D.	3	c Compton, L., b Compton, D.	43
Extras	7	Extras	18
Total	85	Total	186

Runs at the fall of each wicket—

	1	2	3	4	5	6	7	8	9	10
1st Innings	3	4	59	63	66	66	67	74	82	85
2nd Innings	3	41	41	46	46	48	99	129	129	186

BOWLING ANALYSIS

	O.	M.	R.	W.		O.	M.	R.	W.
W. E. Bowes	16	4	34	4	W. E. Bowes	12	4	18	0
A. Coxon	10	1	29	3	A. Coxon	8	3	19	0
J. H. Wardle	4	1	11	0	T. F. Smailes	10	2	53	0
T. F. Smailes	3	0	11	0	J. H. Wardle	36	16	66	7
E. P. Robinson	12.5	1	36	3	E. P. Robinson	29	6	64	3
N. W. D. Yardley	2	0	2	0	T. F. Smailes, bowled 2 no balls				

YORKSHIRE

First Innings	O.	M.	R.	W.	Second Innings	O.	M.	R.	W.
W. J. Edrich	7	1	13	2	W. J. Edrich	7	1	18	1
L. Gray	5	0	14	0	L. Gray	9	3	11	0
J. A. Young	16	5	28	4	J. A. Young	24	6	78	5
D. C. S. Compton	9.5	2	23	4	D.C.S Compton	7.3	1	28	3
					R. W. V. Robins	10	3	23	1
					J. D. Robertson	2	0	10	0

The scorecard for Bill Bowes' benefit match at Headingley, midsummer 1947; Yorkshire were well beaten by that season's champions Middlesex.

Last seasons 1946-48

Courtesy of Michael Ellison:
his grandfather Allan Bailey collected the signatures of the
Yorkshire and Middlesex teams on headed notepaper of the Sun Inn
in the Wasburn Valley, west of Harrogate, after they played a benefit game
for Bill Bowes in 1947. Was Hutton at the bottom because
he was not one for signing autographs?

The Middlesex Championship-winning team of 1947.
Back (l to r): Ian Bedford, Alexander Thompson, Laurie Gray, Leslie Compton,
John Robertson, Sydney Brown, Jack Young. Front: Bill Edrich, George Mann,
Walter Robins, Jim Sims, Denis Compton.

99

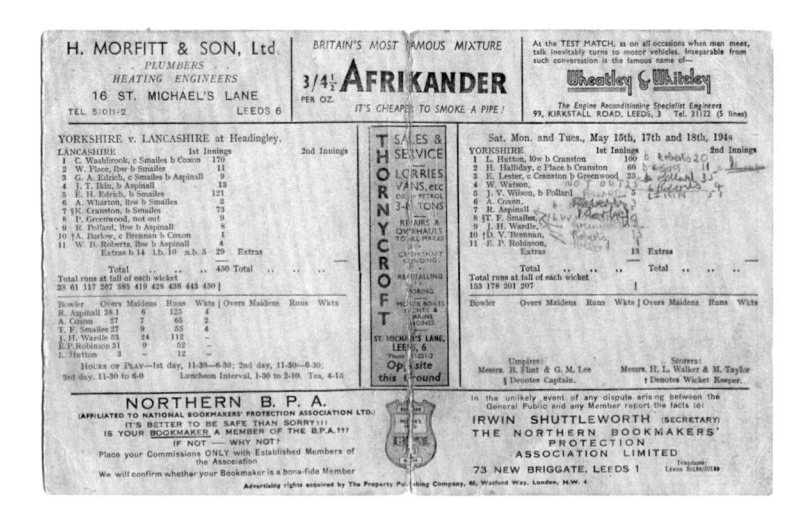

Front and back of the Yorkshire-Lancashire scorecard at Headingley, May 1948, the first Roses match without Sellers for a generation; Smailes captained instead.

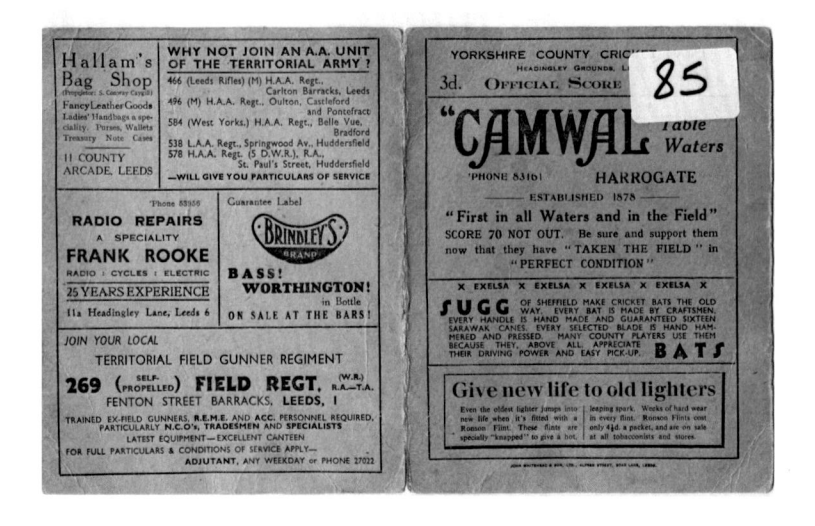

start, 'and I returned to the dressing room a very much sadder man. If I was not a little wiser it was not the fault of Mr Brian Sellers.' In private or in public, whoever it was, Sellers 'set the highest possible standard'. It worked; in ten years Wardle progressed from newcomer, so anxious not to be late that he arrived first, to Ashes-winning left-arm spin bowler. Perhaps he had progressed too far. The way he used Sellers' first name, or his name with title, 'Mr Brian Sellers', in his memoir – and that he was so liberal with private or semi-public conversations – all implied a self-confidence; perhaps an over-confidence. Sellers had left the field, just about – he would play for North Yorkshire aristocrat Sir William Worsley at Hovingham Hall in July 1952, against the Arabs, who included such grandees of cricket as Gubby Allen and Jim Swanton; and as late as 1958 for MCC at his old school. The second, longer half of Sellers' service for the Yorkshire club was beginning; as committee man. Sellers had gone from middle man between the workers and employers to one of the employers; and his record and personality made him powerful even before he took office as chairman of the cricket committee, like his father, in 1959. In 1949, when Fred Trueman made his debut for the Yorkshire first team, Wardle told him: 'There's only one fellow you have to look out for round here. His name is Sellers. Nobody else matters.' To a fellow player, Wardle gave no hint of friendly first name familiarity. Sellers was a man 'to look out for'.

'How right he was,' Trueman recalled in old age.

Chapter Ten
The Wardle Affair

Our contemporaries are constantly excited by two conflicting passions: they want to be led, and they wish to remain free.
Alexis de Tocqueville, Democracy in America

The facts of the Wardle affair are that on Wednesday 30 July 1958, the first day of Yorkshire's match at Bramall Lane, after a meeting of the cricket committee, the county told Wardle and then the world that the club would 'not be calling on his services after the end of the season'. Wardle took eight wickets in the match as Yorkshire beat Somerset by an innings. Wardle bowled most overs for Yorkshire in the match; and indeed that season; and the three seasons before that. In fact Wardle had bowled the most, or second most, overs for the county each season since 1947.

Wardle asked to, and was allowed to, stand down from Yorkshire's next match, at Old Trafford, starting Saturday 2 August. On the Monday, the *Daily Mail* ran the first of three articles in three days in Wardle's name, telling his side of the story and what he thought of the club. The MCC dropped him from their touring party to Australia and he never played first-class cricket in England again. He was 35.

Just as you can follow a river from the sea to the dales and the moors to its source, so in a tragic or complicated or simply a human story like Wardle's you can go back years. To the beginning of his time with Yorkshire, if you like. The impressionable young man who wanted to do well began learning how to play for Yorkshire under Sellers. Did Sellers do a thorough enough job of planting the club culture in him? And even if he did, did Wardle understand that the discipline was for his own good, and the good of all, and not simply because Sellers was like a sergeant major, someone you had to obey because of his rank? And even then, did Wardle apply the discipline to himself – always the surest sort of discipline – and did the captains after Sellers keep the discipline? Once Wardle's three articles forced these questions into the open, plenty of people said not; even the captain that Wardle played under longest. Norman Yardley wrote that he never found Wardle easy to handle, 'but we never had major difficulties'. That did beg the question, what difficulties *did* they have? Many meanwhile said Yardley had been too easy-going. Even Yardley: 'I hate waving the big stick of discipline and somehow I can't get it into my head that it should be necessary in a game of cricket.'

After Yardley retired in 1955, Billy Sutcliffe, Herbert's son, was captain for two unsuccessful years; then Ron Burnet, the second team captain, in

1958. If, presumably, the causes of Wardle's sacking lay partly with the player, partly the club, who was responsible, of all those at the club in Wardle's years?

Just as in a fraud you follow the money and in a murder mystery you do well to find who was nearest the victim, a good question to ask is: who decided to sack Wardle, 'the surprise of the first order', according to Jim Swanton in the *Daily Telegraph* on 31 July. Swanton quoted Sellers: 'There was no indication of this happening on Sunday [27 July] when I helped to pick the England party for Australia. It was a lightning decision. I knew nothing about it before this afternoon. He will be good enough for England but not Yorkshire.' While we cannot read too much into the fact that Sellers said nothing against Wardle – Swanton may not have asked – it's striking how uninformed Sellers claimed to be about his own club. Sellers had indeed been one of three – Freddie Brown and Doug Insole were the others – who chose the 17 for Australia, with the five regular selectors: Les Ames, Tom Dollery, Wilf Wooller and England captain Peter May, chaired by Gubby Allen. If Sellers did know the sacking was coming, his county committee would know he was lying. In January Sellers had been named the next Yorkshire chairman, to take over from Clifford Hesketh in January 1959. Was Hesketh (described witheringly by the *Daily Mail* as a '61-year-old retired colliery official from Barnsley') the type to take such a decision ('the biggest cricket sensation for years', the *Daily Mail* called it) without checking with Sellers? If Sellers had known of the firing, the weekend before Yorkshire did it, but did not warn the MCC selectors, before they hired Wardle for the winter, they could reasonably ask, why not? We can at least speculate that by pleading ignorance, and an implied lack of influence inside his own club, Sellers was telling the smallest lie he could. If Sellers knew what Yorkshire were about to do to Wardle; if, as in Australia in November 1947, he was caught between two masters, he chose Yorkshire. He would not trust the MCC with Yorkshire's business; someone would tell others and the gossip would spread across the small world of English cricket, and into the press. Yorkshire would lose face, and control of their affairs.

In his first article Wardle described how, 'pent up and angry' he sought answers from Hesketh at Bramall Lane. Hesketh hardly came across as strong-willed ('the chairman took out a statement he had prepared and read out the club's reasons for getting rid of me'). Wardle quoted to *Mail* readers Sellers' comment about the 'snap' decision. In fact, Hesketh told him, the committee had considered Wardle weeks earlier when they had 'compulsorily retired' two less senior former England men, Frank Lowson and Bob Appleyard. While the cricket committee minutes have nothing to say about Wardle in 1958, until the sacking, minutes are only the face that a committee wants to show to the world. As early as July 1949, according to the selection committee minutes Yardley and Sellers warned the player Alec Coxon about his 'conduct'; a year later the club sacked him for 'misbehaviour'. As Sellers was willing to do such unpleasant work – and no doubt the other committee members were glad to let him – it's hard to believe he knew as little about Wardle as he pretended to.

Norman Yardley as Yorkshire captain.
Back (l to r): Raymond Illingworth, Frank Lowson, Bob Appleyard, Brian Close, Roy Booth, Fred Trueman. Front: Vic Wilson, Willie Watson, Yardley, Leonard Hutton, Billy Sutcliffe, Johnny Wardle.

As Wardle told his side of the story, it was also striking how much Sellers featured in it. Hesketh complained that Wardle had 'the wrong attitude' and swore on the field. Wardle didn't deny it to the *Mail*, but implied most players swore too. He recalled Trent Bridge in 1947, his 'second or third' match for Yorkshire (in fact his eleventh).

Brian Sellers the noted disciplinarian was my captain and I looked up to him in a manner befitting a colt. We were fielding close to each other – he was in the gully and I was at cover. We both went to field the same ball. As I reached it I heard Sellers shout 'right'. The next thing I knew he had stumbled into me and fallen over me; in the famed Sellers manner he severely reprimanded me with 'when I say right, leave the ... ball alone, you silly young ....'; the words were right, believe me. So why pick on me for the use of bad language in the field.

In a more prudish era, the *Mail* left the actual swear words out. That players, who might otherwise have worked in mines or factories, swore, could hardly came as a surprise; that the captain did, might have shocked. While good manners never took a wicket, they mattered to the Yorkshire club. As so often in this story, this attitude dated from Lord Hawke, who wrote in 1904 that 'the moral character of my men is of infinitely more importance than their form'.

Sellers cast a shadow over Wardle's case. Norman Yardley was 'too nice', Wardle said; players took advantage and 'things began to slide'; although Wardle did not spell it out, he meant a slide in discipline from Sellers' time. Another little story showed how Sellers was keeping his eye on Wardle. At a cricket quiz the previous winter, someone had asked what Wardle thought of Burnet, the new captain. Wardle replied diplomatically enough: Burnet was 39, the captain of the second team and a newcomer to the firsts (much like Sellers had been); but, he might be worth his weight in gold if he pulled the team together. A few weeks later Burnet showed Wardle a newspaper cutting about the speech: 'Burnet told me that Brian Sellers, Yorkshire's former captain had passed it on to him.' Wardle saw Burnet was 'displeased', as any cricketer called a 'passenger' in print would be. More subtly, Wardle evidently felt at liberty to hold and (worse) give opinions. To the club, this was dangerous and presumptuous; and it had bothered Sellers enough for him to keep the offending article and let Burnet know about it. Sellers used to speak far more rudely, without fee, to cricketing and other audiences. John Stanley, as secretary of the Leeds Chartered Accountants Students Society at this time, invited him to speak at their annual dinner, 'and I recall his reference to Nasser as 'that pillock in Egypt' was received with much cheering'.

Wardle, from some of his arguments, might have sounded like an ally of Sellers; because far from being undisciplined, Wardle presented himself as the voice of discipline, unheeded, for instance when he called for a player curfew (and cursing when late to bed players dropped catches the next day). When Yorkshire were plainly faltering on the field in 1957, Swanton among others printed the then novel idea that Yorkshire should make Sellers team manager. Sellers, whether off his own bat or by permission of the committee, was already doing some geeing-up from a distance. 'Get stuck in,' said his telegram in July 1957 to The Oval, where Yorkshire collapsed to an innings defeat against champions Surrey. Wardle's most vivid and hurtful point – hurtful whether it was true or not – struck at those in power at the club: 'A rot has set in with Yorkshire and its committee and it is eating away at the greatest county club in the world.' 'Rot' off the field spread onto the field. Wardle sought reform; or put another way, a return to the Sellers days.

Sellers however was one of the regime that had chosen the unsuccessful captains; and, in his third article, Wardle raised how Yorkshire had not chosen Hutton, captain of England, as their captain. Much later – well after Yorkshire sacked *him*, the season after Wardle – Burnet spoke of whether Hutton wanted to be Yorkshire captain, after Yardley retired. Some said not. Burnet said Hutton did, 'certain of it. Norman Yardley and Brian Sellers said – well, he isn't considering the side at all, he is just collecting hundreds.' In passing, here is one more piece of evidence that Sellers had a say in the important personnel decisions – and what Sellers decided, happened. To Wardle, not making Hutton captain was the 'biggest blunder'. Sellers could not tolerate such criticism, let alone sympathise.

Other critics, outside Yorkshire, were saying much the same; Wardle was simply more informed. Nottinghamshire's Australian spinner Bruce Dooland in a column in July 1957 asked why the 'great White Rose' was so 'wilted'. Yorkshire finished third that season, to Surrey, champions for the sixth time; a feat rivalled only by Yorkshire in Sellers' time, as many noted. In August 1956, Dooland answered his own question; what was the secret of Surrey under captain Stuart Surridge: 'Surridge has something of

Surrey captain Stuart Surridge: the Sellers of the 1950s?

the Brian Sellers type of leadership. He is never beaten, he refuses to give in and he expected 100 per cent from every man under him.' In his memoir Laker, part of Surrey's record-breaking side, suggested that 'in many ways Surridge was the Brian Sellers of the 1950s'; each man was only a moderate batsman, a blessing in disguise, as they could devote themselves to captaincy. Trueman in old age recalled that in the 1950s he found much lingering resentment among other counties against the Yorkshire of the 1930s; and in 1949, Bill Edrich in a column said what others thought; that the 'Tykes' had been champions 'far too often for the general good of the Championship'. Otherwise, the rise of Surrey and (relative) fall of Yorkshire meant that Sellers' reputation stayed high. Yorkshire in the mid-1950s had a strong team – as strong as any, commentators pointed out. The failing, as Wardle argued, lay in the leadership, on the field and off. In his first article on the Wardle sacking, Swanton made a similar point: 'Since 1946 the spirit of Yorkshire cricket has changed ...' In other words, Yorkshire's decline in playing standards dated from the end of Sellers' playing time. The argument lay in who was at fault; and, more to the point, who had to go, to restore the missing team spirit.

Anyone interested, then, could see Wardle as a victim; or as part of the problem of a team not pulling together. Few saw both sides. Cassandra in the *Daily Mirror*, one of the most famous columnists of his time, was one. He showed sympathy for Wardle's dismissal (in the 'best headmaster-bad boy tradition'), then condemned him for bursting into print, 'with a school boy scribbling that does him no credit'. Cassandra's verdict mattered more than most, because such leading columnists mirrored and led public opinion at the same time, and many readers never turned to the sports pages. A year later, when Burnet 'resigned' (the 'passenger' captain that Yorkshire in effect had chosen over Wardle) newspapers quoted Wardle: 'anyway I had better say nowt more for fear of putting my foot in it all over again'. By going to a newspaper in August 1958, Wardle had indeed put his foot in it.

The very power of his case – that plainly had been brewing in him for years – caused offence. The truth hurt. The stink was big enough for Cassandra to notice. However by giving his story only to the *Daily Mail*, Wardle was keeping it from every other daily. Journalists would resent that; most came down against him. Wardle brought another issue into the affair; Yorkshire could, less hypocritically than the newspapers denied their scoop, pose as the victim. Yardley for example complained of 'washing of dirty linen in public'. Swanton deplored what had become a 'sordid wrangle'. The club won the public relations contest. Other counties' interest in Wardle – by Nottinghamshire for one – came to nothing. Sellers said little or nothing; he did not have to, because others such as Yardley made the committee's case for it. But for what Yardley called Wardle's 'bitter words', Yorkshire would have looked the ungrateful employer, sacking their senior professional without explaining why, to himself or the public, which Wardle could reasonably feel implied something was wrong with him; but what? Yorkshire never said in these cases, because once an employer gave reasons, it was treating the worker as an equal, and risked giving away knowledge about itself, at worst looking foolish.

In November 1959, at a meeting at Lord's of the MCC advisory county cricket committee – Sellers was there with Yorkshire secretary John Nash – players writing for the press cropped up. It was significant that, according to the minutes, two of the most dictatorial heads of counties had their say. Wilf Wooller said the Glamorgan contract covered it, and 'none of his players had stepped out of line'; which said much about how Wooller saw players speaking their mind, and behaving generally. Sellers felt that any article written by players should be vetted by the county secretary. 'He indicated that an eminent amateur cricketer had written in a national newspaper advising the Yorkshire CCC as to whom their next captain should be and he felt that there should be some sort of legislation to prevent this sort of thing. All seemed well if articles were vetted.'

Evidently it irked Sellers that players outside Yorkshire went into print with their opinions about the club; he wanted them to mind their own business. Was he asking that the secretaries of the other 16 counties censor whatever their players said about Yorkshire, or did he want the right to censor? Did Sellers or anyone around the table remember he had been free with his opinions about Hammond, 13 years before?!

Yorkshire committee men in a press photograph during the Wardle affair, August 1958; Brian Sellers third from left.

At least Wooller gave contracts to players. Yorkshire gave players 'gentlemen's agreements' from summer to summer, allowing the club to give a month's notice to anyone; as they did to Wardle. Herbert Sutcliffe, in reply to Wardle in the *Daily Mirror*, said that Wardle had broken his contract by going into print without vetting by the county secretary. Ray Illingworth parted with the club in 1968 because he wanted more than a 'gentleman's agreement'. Here was another example of the club keeping things vague, so it could do as it pleased. Illingworth's move - to leave Yorkshire and, as importantly, captain Leicestershire to success - was a sign of the changing times.

In 1958, the Wardle affair not only rid Yorkshire of a trouble-maker; it sent a message to the other players: step out of line, and be cast out; not only from Yorkshire, but any prospect of playing for England, or another county, even. Whether Yorkshire recovered their team spirit without Wardle, or did better in the 1960s merely because Surrey declined, did not matter, even if you could measure such intangibles. Yorkshire rid itself of what Sutcliffe in the *Mirror* called its 'soft underbelly' of the past few seasons, in contrast to the 'old die hard spirit and urge to win that was the hallmark of our play throughout the 1930s'. With Sellers as chairman, Yorkshire entered the 1960s with the 1930s in charge. Was that the new leadership Wardle had wished for in the *Daily Mail*? He had said in his third and final article:

There is so much wrong to be right that it is a wonder that the committee have got away with it for so long. There must be an outcry from the good folk who make up the county's 12,000 members. They have been extremely patient in these dark years. But the pot is simmering. Sooner or later it is going to boil over. I urge them to be en masse at the annual meeting of the club. That is the only way they will ever find out what is going on.

Eventually, and in Sellers' time, they would.

Chapter Eleven
The Sixties

Some men are much better and wiser than others, but experience seems to show that hardly any man is so much better or wiser than others that he can permanently stand the test of irresponsible power over them.
LT Hobhouse, Liberalism (1911)

Why did Sellers, and not Herbert Sutcliffe for instance, become chairman in 1959? Being a leader on the field did not mean, in any sport, that you could lead as well, or at all well, in a committee. Sellers was however highly qualified. He was used to meetings, as a Test selector while a player, before he joined the Yorkshire committee. In July 1939 the *Derby Evening Telegraph* reported Sellers left the match at Chesterfield at 4 pm on the Saturday, to pick England's team for the Second Test against West Indies, that would start the following Saturday. *The Times*, previewing the season in April 1959, noted Sellers' take-over, calling him 'dynamic and forthright'. Were they codewords for tyrannical? Even if they were, the *Times* commented that 'an influence such as his seems to be just what Yorkshire need'. *The Times* correctly named Yorkshire as one of Surrey's challengers; Yorkshire became champions to end Surrey's seven year run. When Yorkshire famously won their last match to clinch the Championship at Hove, by scoring at a good seven runs an over, Sellers told the press: 'I think it is a magnificent performance by a young, inexperienced side. I said earlier in the season that I didn't expect to win the Championship until 1961, but I am delighted to be able to eat those words.' Success, as always, disarmed any critics.

Sellers simply put the time in. He and some of his former players were among the mourners at George Hirst's funeral at Huddersfield, in May 1954, for instance. When Sellers and others wrote to accept an invitation from Lord's to be a member of the MCC's 1961 inquiry into the future of first-class cricket, they said when they could attend meetings: 'Any weekday,' Sellers wrote, and not Saturday or Sunday. As Swanton wrote of the inquiry's 20 members – by later standards ludicrously top-heavy with distinguished players and old-guard administrators: these were 'true amateurs ... in that they give countless hours of free and selfless service to the game'. It's telling that in an age of professionals, in sport and workplaces generally, the very word 'amateur' has become a sneer; to do something not for money (except expenses, maybe) but for the love of it is old-fashioned, even mad. In truth amateurism (if, like all things, done well) had a point. While amateurs in politics, as in the 101 civic bodies that made England what it was, were a select club, because few could afford to do something for nothing, they answered not to shareholders, the press, or public even, but to themselves; their conscience, if you like. They did what they thought was best; and if they tended to be old and conservative, even conservatives had to manage change. They only argued over the details, the timing and pace of change – and argued over and over without deciding anything, it seemed, as Lord's set up one committee and inquiry after another.

In August 1957, for instance, Lord's named Sellers in a committee to consider the place of amateurs in first-class cricket. Looking back, the members – let alone the chairman, the Duke of Norfolk – were laughably one-sided. They were holders of offices: Lord's insiders such as Rait Kerr and Gubby Allen; the old such as Harry Altham; and current players, such as England captain Peter May. Most came from the south; of the 13 on the committee, only Sellers and the Lancashire secretary Geoffrey Howard had northern connections. All had played as amateurs and stood for amateurism. Whole books have been written about these years when English cricket tortuously gave up amateurism. Most are guilty of assuming that because professionalism – that is, paid play for all – came in 1963, the end of amateurism was inevitable, and right; and its defenders were behind the times, even stupid.

At the committee's first meeting on Wednesday afternoon, 9 October 1957, Sellers was emphatic (in the words of the minutes) in wishing to send the best MCC tour side; even if that meant paying some. That implied Sellers was ready to compromise on the pure amateur principle, for the sake of a strong England abroad. Likewise in the second meeting on Thursday afternoon, 28 November, Sellers reminded the committee that it had agreed to separate the issue of tours (when amateurs might get help) and seasons at home, 'as it would be a tragedy if the amateur was run out of the game'. As that suggested, the committee was looking for ways to keep the amateur in play. Indeed, a memo for the committee beforehand set out the aim of encouraging *more* amateurs to play first-class cricket, 'and bring with them the leadership, drive and enterprise traditionally associated with the Amateur game'.

The wish of Lord's to revive amateurism had a hitch: reality. Few if any were playing cricket purely for the love of it: they were signing bats, putting their name to press articles (including Peter May) and adverts; altogether making a business of being an amateur cricketer. Hence Gubby Allen spoke of the 'real amateur' and the Duke of Norfolk of the 'genuine amateur', which implied some amateurs were fake. The committee's report in February 1958 admitted that unlike 50 years before amateurs could not afford to play first-class cricket at their own expense.

When Burnet 'resigned' in October 1959, Sellers told Frank Rostron of the *Daily Express*: 'There is absolutely no prejudice against professionals and all candidates will be judged solely on their merits. The *Express* named Derek Blackburn of Bradford and Mike Crawford of Doncaster as two possible amateur captains; Yorkshire however chose one of their older professionals, Vic Wilson. Why did Sellers go against a tradition of amateur captains? Presumably, because there was no amateur with the character of Sellers, or Burnet, to lead the other ten, and with enough basic playing ability. As ever, what Yorkshire did was only half the story; what other counties were doing was the other half. Other counties had gone over to a captain from among their professionals, with success. An all-professional team would always make more runs or take more wickets than a team of ten professionals carrying an amateur captain. Unless Yorkshire wanted to be also-rans, they had to follow, and give up an amateur captain.

County clubs had to make such decisions; while the MCC, setting policy for all, was spinning out questions for years, decades even, rather than coming to a decision that might offend some. One trick of the MCC was to stack a committee with people that thought the same way; the 1957 committee on amateurs for example merely 'consulted' some professionals over lunch. The 1961 inquiry on the future of first-class cricket did draw on a slightly wider spectrum of cricket, as it included old professionals such as Bill Bowes, and Alec Bedser. *The Times* described the 20 as 'mostly men of progressive ideas who are not afraid to express them'. However, they were also 'some of the game's most dauntless talkers', which brought the risk of no end of talk without agreement. The inquiry duly worried away at amateurs. On Thursday 8 February 1962, Sellers said that he 'was forced to the conclusion that the time was coming when the status of the amateur would have to be waived'. And on Tuesday 29 May 1962, Sellers agreed with the previous speaker Walter Robins: '... that the dividing line between the amateur and the professional was very slender and he felt that unless we moved with the times cricket would fall into disrepute. Public opinion he said would ignore the distinction in the first class game and would accept all players as cricketers.' Sellers, speaking of 'time' and 'the times', was implying that regardless of personal preference or even what was good for the game, those in authority were helpless against wider social trends. He was thus altogether more realistic than a reactionary such as MCC secretary Ronnie Aird, who at an earlier meeting argued amateurs would play more if only given the chance, and that counties should *cut* the number of professionals.

The authorities were helpless because the game was going broke; only about half a dozen counties even after economies could hope to break even in an average year. At the inquiry's meeting on Thursday 23 November 1961, Sellers stressed spectator appeal. 'He said that in Yorkshire his committee was coming round to the opinion that there was a surfeit of counties today and that the public should get less. He did not think that one-day cricket would attract the public though he had no objection to the introduction of a knockout competition on a one-day basis as an experiment.' C.A.F.Hastilow the chairman of Warwickshire proposed, and Sellers seconded, that from 1963 each first-class county play 28 three-day County Championship matches (some were playing 32) and 'a knockout competition to include certain minor counties ... on the basis of one-day single innings matches'. Donald Carr and Gubby Allen – in other words, the MCC – put forward an amendment to defer the one-day competition; that lost, five votes to seven. The Hastilow resolution was then agreed without a vote – to preserve the myth that everyone at Lord's agreed on everything, true to the idea that disunity was a sign of weakness that critics could exploit. Through such dry acts of a committee, and far from willingly, came the crucial first reform of first-class cricket, that became the Gillette Cup, and that led to a Sunday league, international one-dayers, T20 and cricket as the 21st century knows it.

It was a truly British act of evolution, like the 1832 Reform Act. Those in authority gave way: too much, complained some; not enough, complained others. Sellers was one of those at the centre of authority; he had become a committee member of the MCC in May 1960, for three years. Some of the 16 other members had been county captains in his playing days: E.R.T.Holmes and Robbins. Why was Sellers one of the trusted few, given that he had 'blotted his copybook' in Australia in 1946, and was notoriously 'forthright'? There was more than one side to Sellers. The side the public saw was 'the blunt, hail-fellow-well-met Yorkshireman with a habit of addressing folk as 'me old cock sparrer" as the long-time journalist E.M.Wellings put it. Sellers could fit into various company; or, to be less charitable, he could put on faces, and voices (broad Yorkshire, or posher). As Wellings noted: 'If he sometimes gave the impression of being a bull in a china shop, he could when necessary act with tact and diplomacy.' Surviving letters of his to Lord's prove this. In July 1957, Sellers wrote to Ronnie Aird: 'Dear Ronny, I shall be delighted to serve on the sub-committee – anything to help any time will be a pleasure. Hope all is well with you. Best wishes from Brian.' Those few words show Sellers entirely at ease with Lord's and on first-name terms; Doug Insole and Alec Hastilow, to name two others who sent acceptance letters, signed with their full names. And on 30 December 1959, sending Yorkshire's views on amateur status ahead of a meeting, Sellers wrote in the same 'Dear Ronny' vein: 'Yorkshire have no further comments to make to this meeting. Sorry to be so late. Best wishes, yours ever Brian.' In return Lord's was as cheery as it could be: 'My dear Brian, I will see that his Grace [the Duke of Norfolk] is informed of the possibility of your late arrival.' Contrast Sellers' good relations with Lord's with a man who outwardly had much in common with him, Wilfred Wooller, of Glamorgan. In April 1961 for example Wooller began a letter to Aird: 'I have always thought the amateur status standing committee a stupid idea but I am now quite certain it is stark raving mad.' Aird replied that Wooller had written 'a great many pretty offensive letters to me in the past'.

Faced by someone in authority who can bully some – usually those below him in rank – and be nice to others, we might resent them as hypocrites. While such men might be calculating in their dealings with others, which again we might resent as falseness, Sellers was a man with more than one setting on his control panel. After Yorkshire won the Championship in 1962 (under Vic Wilson) and 1963 (in Brian Close's first season as captain) Yorkshire came only fifth in 1964 and by August 1965 were out of the running again. In his 1987 autobiography, Boycott told what happened next. Sellers 'thrust his head round the dressing-room door at Headingley and told everyone he would see them individually next morning':

His words were frequently undiluted Anglo-Saxon, straight to the point and – as near as made absolutely no difference – the law of the club. One by one the victims were summoned into the presence, one by one they returned with long faces and a distinct trace of scorch-marks round the ears ....
I was the last to be called in ... Sellers was efficient and remorseless. I eventually found myself quaking in front of him, mesmerised by his gaze over the half-glasses that made him look like a Dickensian headmaster. I expected a volley, but Sellers simply said, 'Now then, what's the matter?' It was clear from the question and his tone that Sellers knew I was suffering ... I told him I couldn't work it out myself ... Sellers was understanding personified. He suggested I was trying too hard and had become too tense, and told me to go out in every innings to the end of the season and concentrate on relaxing and taking my time. Take an hour to get used to the pitch and the bowlers and then just play naturally – and don't worry if you get out. It wasn't what I expected but it was certainly what I needed.

Hutton, 30 years before, had gained from much the same advice. Three weeks later Boycott made his celebrated 146 in the Gillette Cup final at Lord's, as Yorkshire won their first one-day trophy.

Partly thanks to Sellers, county cricket had given up amateurism and accepted one-dayers. Sellers like other officials now had to urge his players to embrace it and so excel at it – and keep excelling. That may

Yorkshire team, 1966, at Bradford Park Avenue:
back (l to r): GL Alcock (masseur), Philip Sharpe, Doug Padgett, Don Wilson, Tony Nicholson, John Hampshire, Geoffrey Boycott. Front: Jimmy Binks, Fred Trueman, Brian Close (captain), Raymond Illingworth, Ken Taylor.

seem odd as Yorkshire players, including Sellers, had learned in one-day leagues; although as county players who often aspired to play for England, they may have felt that three-day matches set them apart from league cricketers. A longer cricket match (or book) is not necessarily better quality. Sellers, in old age like many, metaphorically shook his head at how unadventurous cricket took hold in the one-day game:

Containment today, not experiment. They have a theory that a spinner can't spin a new ball. Rubbish. Rhodes would've given 'em three sixes to get their wickets. Eighteen runs a wicket – that's not bad.

In Sunday League games, where overall scoring rates might only be four runs an over, 18 runs might have been bad. However, with such suggestions, Sellers was decades ahead of his time:

Why not experiment today in one-day cricket. No-one chases early on – the openers don't. No-one straight drives past or over the bowler's head. It amazes me, because nowadays you don't need to put a man out there. Why, when we faced Wally Hammond we always pulled in mid-on, mid-off closer to the bowler (the only people in danger were the umpire and the bowler). Wally's great strokes were past the bowler and we had to counter them ... He used it because it is the shortest way to the boundary – the fastest way. Why don't players use it today.

There's nothing new under the sun. Sellers' ideas are now the norm in one-day cricket – so-called pinch hitters, slow bowlers taking the pace off the ball, extreme attention to detail in the field – and were only waiting to be applied; it took captains with the knowledge and the self-confidence to defy convention.

This does beg the main problem for any eminent sportsman who goes into club management or player coaching; how does he make a success of new tasks; drawing on his reputation, without boring younger men with his 'in my day' stories, or sticking to outdated ways of thinking? In a 1961 book, *Fast Fury*, Fred Trueman spoke of how a match at Bradford (that is, nearest Sellers' home in Bingley) never went by without Sellers 'breezing in': 'If we are not doing very well he never hesitates to remind us (very forcibly) of the fact and say what we ought to try and do to put things right.' As Trueman was still a player at the time, he had to tell stories with care. One story however gave an insight into Sellers; when Brian Close crashed his car, damaged his knee (that 'gave him a lot of trouble later on') and had to step down from the team. Trueman told how Sellers 'burst into the room' (he never seemed to enter a room in any other way) 'and exclaimed, nah then, weers Stirling Moss? There were many smiles and Brian Close looked rather sheepish.' As so often, more than one reading of this story is possible. Was Sellers simply lacking in human sympathy? Yet other players had smiled at the comparison of Close (notoriously bad behind the wheel) with a racing driver. Was Sellers showing (by his standards) compassion? as he could have bawled out the senior player for his avoidable injury. Sellers had made a joke of it. 'He was a man among men,' Sidney Fielden recalled in 2016. The story becomes more ominous given Bryan Stott's opinion that Brian Sellers didn't have any trust in Brian Close, as a cricketer; 'he was always expecting that Brian [Close] would do something silly'.

Sellers did good for the club; for instance in July 1960 he got Trueman released from the Gentlemen-Players match at Lord's, while Lancashire, the other leading team in the Championship, did not ask for their leading fast bowler, Brian Statham. Sellers told reporters: 'I don't much care what the Lancashire people think about it.' Yorkshire were doing well; they won the Championship in 1960; came second to Hampshire in 1961; and won again in 1962; and 1963. How did they do it? Crawford White of the *Daily Express* asked Sellers in September 1962. 'I can soon tell thee t'answer,' Sellers replied. Having neatly hinted to readers that Sellers was talking in broad Yorkshire, White then returned to proper English.

We spend a lot of time and brass finding our players. We are a vast county. There are over 500 clubs. Another advantage is that our youngsters are born to competitive league cricket. And their burning ambition is to play for Yorkshire.

These advantages of social geography had applied for generations. 'If our team were wiped out I would guarantee another Yorkshire side on top in five years,' Sellers added, somewhat crassly, as an air crash had indeed wiped out the Manchester United football team in 1958. It all went to show that Yorkshire had everything going for it; the supply of talent was such that 'we have another full team at least of Yorkshire exiles with other county sides'.

And there lay the trouble; the way he kept saying 'we'. As if he were Yorkshire cricket. If Sellers was in error, it was an error that he had grown into, as shown from a story from this time, from Sidney Fielden. Around this time, the future Yorkshire committee man was a young police detective under his sergeant Leonard Bell ('Sellers thought the world of him, called him Ding Dong') at Shipley. The two policemen, and the vicar of Baildon, Horace Pike, would play snooker at the soldiers' and sailors' club at nearby Baildon ('a gentlemen's club, ladies not allowed, only once a year'). At about midnight, 'Sellers would burst through the double doors, and shout, 'which of you [fornicating buggers] is going to play me at snooker?!' That's the type of man he was. Quite funny, is that, the way he used to do that. Everybody used to laugh."

On his earlier beat of Conisborough, near Doncaster, Fielden had become friends with Ellis Robinson, who lived there, and had heard stories about Sellers. Now Fielden was getting to know the man himself, playing doubles at snooker until 2 am or 3 am. As Sellers bustled around the table ('physically very big and strong ... his language was very choice'), using his cue as a stick, because of a stiff hip, Fielden could ask Sellers for stories about Hutton and Verity. As Fielden recalled: 'It was good, wasn't it.' Sellers was, as Fielden said, 'a very impressive man, of course'. Others wanted to be impressed. Sellers, with that habit of theatrical entrances, evidently liked imposing himself. His daughter-in-law Anne agreed about his need to say something when he entered a room, even a shop: 'You always knew he was there.' Did he miss the applause from his years as captain, as he entered and left the field?

Certainly Sellers as chairman used his power over the players. That made them wary. One of them, Bryan Stott, recalled in 2016 "the first time I had anything other than a 'morning Mr Sellers' or whatever". Around 1953, he had Easter leave during his National Service, which meant he could attend the outside nets at Headingley. While he was fielding, 'all of a sudden Brian Sellers appears next to me':

'Now then lad, you are in the air force.' I said, 'Yes Mr Sellers.' He said, are you enjoying it? I said, well, you know, on and off, because we were getting used to square bashing. And chatting there and he was just asking me questions. Are you playing any cricket? We were hoping of course, most of the lads had played good cricket in the air force. We had a good liaison between the RAF and Yorkshire. These were the first words of any nature spoken and not many afterwards. But he was totally in charge.

Stott was one of the 13 capped players, an unusually large number, for the 1962 season. A scene at the April nets became one of the most written-about in Yorkshire history:

… we always used to have Brian Sellers give us a pep talk, he used to come into the dressing room before we started practice and said pull your fingers out and get this championship won. We were all waiting there; he comes into the dressing room, closes the door, he leant against it and looked around [Stott folded his arms as Sellers did], *he says, 'well, there's 13 of you buggers here now, but there won't be at the end of the season'. And walked out, no pep talk, no nothing. Out. I thought; everybody is looking around, hell fire, what is he on about? This is how he was. Bang, this was what he had decided.*

With those few words - the fewer, the more they sank in - Sellers was reminding all that 13 caps were too many, as it kept out new blood (never mind that the club was at fault for giving so many caps). Sellers was thinking of the overall playing health of the club, that the players, understandably selfish, could not. Sellers was making all 13 try harder. In his 1969 autobiography - when he was safely away from Yorkshire - Illingworth, another one of those 13, felt free to analyse the Yorkshire attitude. It was always 'that you play better under pressure'. Some did, Illingworth agreed; 'others need encouragement'. Observant man that he was, observant enough to make a long and successful second career in cricket management and broadcasting, Illingworth added that 'this pressure from the top, the constant awareness that you mustn't fail' was, as far as he could tell at the time, particular to Yorkshire. Was it right? As Illingworth said, 'a lot of disillusioned youngsters' were joining other counties; and indeed men no longer young, such as him. In fairness to Sellers, he let the players know where they stood; would they rather have been in ignorance, or denial? Supply of talent at Yorkshire always had been much greater than the eleven places, raising the odds against making the first eleven. Illingworth had made the Yorkshire first team in his teens; sooner than Verity and Wilfred Rhodes. Sellers as chairman had to think of the club's future, and the interests of future Illingworths. In his third and final *Daily Mail* article, Wardle had complained of a 'terrible feeling of uncertainty hanging over so many' Yorkshire players; men released with years of good cricket in them (Wardle named Watson; he hardly needed to add himself); and young uncapped players wondering if they were better off elsewhere (Doug Padgett, for example). Yet by 1962 Padgett was capped, and had played for England. From a critic's perspective, Sellers was playing on everyone's loyalty to Yorkshire, keeping the workers down, 'treating players as if they were made of wood', in Wardle's vivid phrase. Stott was in the field, at Bristol, when captain Vic Wilson went off to take the news of which two capped players Yorkshire would not keep for next season: 'It was a horrible way of doing business.' That was only how employers in the mills, factories and farms treated their men. Workers at Sellers' printing works remembered it fondly enough. Steve Troth, a teenage apprentice there in the early 1970s, called it 'old school'; workers called the Sellers family directors 'Mr Brian', 'Mr Godfrey', 'Mr David' and 'Mr Andrew'.

Players resisted Sellers' enforcement of what could look like cosmetic, unnecessary standards. In old age, Trueman recalled how an electric shaver company offered him £1000 (a year's pay for a workman in the 1960s) to grow a beard, that they would shave off. Sellers 'went mad': 'You can get that lot shaved off straight away. You haven't asked permission to grow a beard, so get it off. We want no seafaring buggers in here.' What was the problem; would Trueman bowl any less fast, bearded?! Sellers could hardly object to whiskers (after all, W.G.Grace had a beard; Lord Hawke had a moustache) but did mind the sign of independent thinking in Trueman; by this time someone setting an example to juniors. Sellers, as the voice of the club, did not sound open to granting permission for beards; he was demanding a uniform look. A beard – or rather, some men choosing beards, some not – was an offence against team unity, or rather the (as important) appearance of it. Time-keeping, too, was obvious to enforce. In July 1962 Trueman notoriously over-slept and arrived late at the Taunton ground; captain Vic Wilson sent him home. Leaving aside who and what to believe – Trueman was an over-worked and tired victim (Trueman) or a law to himself (others) - Trueman had to drive to Yorkshire to apologise to Sellers and his committee. The club, literally, would not meet its leading player halfway. Sportsmen were not precious and powerful yet.

If the Close affair of 1967 showed anything, it was that Yorkshire were no harsher employers than the MCC. Briefly, Close became captain of England in the summer of 1966. At Edgbaston on 18 August 1967, Warwickshire ended a Championship match on 133 for five, nine short of victory. Yorkshire had bowled 24 overs in 98 minutes – in fact a faster rate than the 16 overs an hour that England had bowled in the most recent Test match. Warwickshire spectators however had taken offence; and John Woodock in the *Times* accused Yorkshire of 'all the known methods of wasting time', such as 'endless consultations' and walking slowly between overs, and generally; everyday 21st century cricket, in other words. The MCC appointed a committee of six under Arthur Gilligan – the 72-year-old president-elect of MCC – that 'severely censured' Close for unfair 'delaying tactics', of the sort that saved or won England many Test matches before and since. In a book the year after, Close recalled how he went outside after the verdict – the southern cricket establishment having relished the chance to take Close, and Yorkshire, down a peg. Sellers, one of the six on the committee, followed him. 'I told him I was ready to quit. Mr Sellers fixed me with that baleful glare which pre-war Yorkshire cricketers tell me reduced strong men to putty in his hands.'

Sellers told Close: 'This isn't the end. You have a job of work to do,' namely captaining England against Pakistan the next day, in the final Test of the summer, that England won. 'Get over there [The Oval] and do it and get stuck in.' (Sellers did like that phrase.) Close was grateful: 'Mr Sellers' sensible words acted as shock treatment.'

Sellers was even more outnumbered as one of the MCC committee of 18 that decided not to pick Close on tour that winter, thus ending his time as England captain. Sellers was outnumbered not only as a backer of Close, but as a cricket man who could appreciate that Close acted at Birmingham for a reason; which the likes of former Conservative prime minister Sir Alec Douglas Home in the chair, and Lieutenant-General Sir Oliver Leese, the 72-year-old former corps commander under Montgomery, would not. Sellers was there because he served three three-year terms at the MCC, retiring eventually in September 1971. Sellers was still relevant; certainly by comparison with the MCC. As time passed, Sellers' playing days were becoming legend. Alan Gibson in the *Times* in May 1967 harked back to how Sellers on a drying, uncovered wicket would put Verity on at once and six fielders around the bat, according to the old Wilfred Rhodes motto: 'If batsman thinks it's spinnin', it's spinnin'.' Again, in August 1967 Gibson used Sellers as a stick to beat the present Yorkshire team with, for not scoring fast enough to take the chance to bowl on a wet pitch. Why so critical? Yorkshire were county champions in 1967; and 1968. However, as times changed, the social geography that made Yorkshire one of the strongest cricketing counties was changing, for the worse. In *The Cricketer* in July 1968, Bill Bowes warned 'the vital basis of Yorkshire cricket is vanishing'. He saw two dangers. First: time limit or limited-overs cricket inside the county was making spin bowlers, 'a traditional strength in Yorkshire cricket', less useful; hence fewer were developing. Second: to be a Yorkshire cricketer was 'no longer the aim of every youngster in the county'; what the club paid was not much more than any other employer. Few showed 'a Boycott-like concentration'. Bowes, a major name in Yorkshire cricket and a journalist, could only sound the alarm. It was asking a lot of any one man, in cricket or any field of life, to resist or alter trends in society – that is to say, what came naturally to many people. Yet if anyone could do something, Sellers could – and in any case, he was the one the club would look to.

Chapter Twelve
When I'm 64: Illingworth and Close

Nobody, but nobody, my friend, had any foreboding that the end was drawing near. Or rather, one did sense something, something haunting, but so vague, so indistinct, that it was not like a presentiment of the extraordinary.
Ryszard Kapuscinski, The Emperor

A clue to where the Yorkshire committee stood politically came, as for so many in sport in that era, over southern Africa. The club was ready in autumn 1967 to take up an invitation to tour Rhodesia – then a white-rule break-away state. 'All we are trying to do is play cricket,' said Sellers. Such was the cry, then and later – at the Moscow Olympics in 1980, and on tours of South Africa in the 1980s until apartheid fell - of the supposedly unpolitical sportsman. The Labour Government objected that Yorkshire would aid the whites-only regime, if it took the hospitality. On 15 September, Sellers' cricket committee voted to pass the matter to the larger general committee, 'in view of the many issues involved' as the committee minutes put it. Three days later came the unanimous vote – again, that MCC-like mania to show unity to the outside world – not to go to Rhodesia. As a sign of what the committee men really thought, Herbert Sutcliffe's dog wore a label on its collar saying 'Yorkshire for Rhodesia' (a political-sounding slogan!?). When reporters asked Sellers about the political pressure, he replied simply: 'Ask Whitehall.' He added: 'It's a great pity that you can't just go and have a game. Anywhere else would have done.' Just as 'if batsman thinks it's spinnin', it's spinnin'', once anyone insisted that you were doing something political, you were political. Other invited English sports clubs had said no to Rhodesia. Sellers was correct; Yorkshire could have picked 'anywhere' from a dozen countries, and over the years the club had: Jamaica in 1935, North America in 1964. At best, Sellers and his committee had been naïve; at worst, they had made themselves look like bigots.

Yorkshire were closing the 1960s much as they closed the 1930s; their successful side near full of England players was if anything too outstanding for its own good. Several ageing men were about to finish at once. By August 1968, Ray Illingworth, having turned 36, and facing competition as an off-spinner from the young Geoff Cope, wanted a three-year contract. Yorkshire, as ever, would not compromise with a player. Illingworth sent a letter of resignation, which made hardly a ripple in the press. In an autobiography the year after, Illingworth described how, an hour after he handed in his letter on the Monday morning, Bill Bowes was asking him about it in the dressing room at Bradford:

Quite clearly there had been no time for Yorkshire to call a committee meeting. I was soon to realise that the decision to release me had been taken by the chairman, Brian Sellers, who declared that if I didn't want to play for them I could go.

Someone evidently told other players what Sellers said exactly. Geoff Boycott quoted it in his own autobiographies: "Brian Sellers said to him: 'If you want to go, then you can fucking well go. Fuck off.' He actually used those words." Leaving aside the bad manners, that Illingworth had to cover up, and who Sellers said it to - as a comment over the 'phone to John Nash the secretary, some suggested - it looked like the same old outcome between employer and worker; as soon as a man sought a better deal for himself, the club threw him out. Sellers was carrying on a tradition that he saw in his first full season, when Yorkshire released another ageing player, Percy Holmes. In old age, Sellers described the county cap as a 'bond' between the county and player; and if the player got his 'ticket', 'he always got 18 months' notice' (not true; Johnny Wardle didn't). Sellers claimed that the 'end of season' dismissal changed when Yorkshire finished with Holmes in August 1933:

... he had bad knees, that was the only reason, a question of fitness, you see. Well, Percy got his ticket in the second or third week of August. He didn't complain about it. The Lancashire and Birmingham leagues would have jumped at him. But by the time he got his ticket they had all signed up their pro's, so poor Percy's bad luck changed the procedure. But it was still a gentleman's agreement that players would know if they were to get their ticket by July 1 - that was the deadline.

We can query whether 'poor Percy' had bad luck or whether in fact the club chose to do what suited it, as soon as Holmes began to flag. And did Holmes not complain because complaining would have done him no good?! The press took the club's side. The *Yorkshire Post* at the time reported that the committee 'had been influenced by the desire to give the batsman a full opportunity to make arrangements for league cricket or a coaching engagement for next season'. Either Sellers' memory was at fault, or the committee had given Holmes less 'opportunity' than it claimed.

The club in fairness did have its own interests to protect. It wanted only the best first eleven, and a flow of players into that eleven. Significantly, in his interview in old age, Sellers went from that Holmes story to the 'poaching' of young players, 'a cause of great anxiety for Yorkshire':

It cost about £1000 to bring a youngster up to first team standard. There was a lot of underhand work went on by counties - and there's a lot still going on today, but now it's among the players themselves. The hot poker suddenly arrived when Raymond Illingworth asked for a three-year contract or he'd want his release. He was a forward-thinker, before his time, you couldn't blame him. But y'see, it was new - it upset the bond of trust, caused an imbalance in the Yorkshire tradition ... money has killed the game - it is very difficult today - you've got to have a squad (as you say) of about 16 or 18 players with one-day games. Cricket has changed and we can't change it, we can't criticise it.

While cricketers like any workers looking for the best deal were to Sellers 'underhand', he could view Illingworth with sympathy, and as part of a wider movement. At the time, however, Illingworth had to become one more unwanted player having to leave. Or rather, the player had simply not agreed to the employer's deal; most did. In a talk to the Northern Cricket Society in October 1960, Sellers significantly linked the club's conditions of employment, and other counties' recruitment. Other counties had approached several young players, and approached capped players from time to time, but the players knew which side their bread was buttered, he said: 'No other county consistently gave benefits as good as Yorkshire's.' In other words, if a player stayed with Yorkshire, and behaved, a benefit season would give him more money in the end than another county could. Indeed, Illingworth had accepted that deal; he took a benefit in 1965 of £6500, a six-figure sum by 21st century standards.

Players, then, had more choice than they let on, and Yorkshire did have its investment to protect (although as always in sport, the local clubs truly brought on talented youth, that the paying club took credit for). As Sellers told the October 1957 annual dinner of the Bradford League, Yorkshire was not blind to other counties offering a young player a three- or five-year contract. Yorkshire, he said, would not stand in the way of a player that wanted to leave. If we were to put it less charitably, the club did not want to raise its bid in the market for labour. Yorkshire felt the other county ought to ask for permission. 'There is going to be a dust-up about this,' Sellers said. 'It will be done very quietly but it will be done.' Again, as with MCC, we see the mania in cricket for the pretence of a happy family, and raising conflicts privately. Yorkshire took offence at 'poaching' because it would never poach; it only wanted men born in the county. Once it dropped that custom, it would become like any other county. Sellers was modern enough to understand that players wanted more money and longer contracts; and old-fashioned enough to resist. Sellers resisted any change that might take power from the committee and give it to the captain, or the other players. In his 2014 book *The Corridor of Certainty*, Boycott described selection committee meetings during a home Championship match: 'Sellers would call Closey off the field and summon him into the meeting.' Brian Close did not know his next team, because 'the committee would just ask Brian his opinion and then dismiss him while they made the decisions'. Besides the actual power resting with the committee, and its chairman, we should note - as Boycott took care to show - the way Sellers used that power, to 'summon' and 'dismiss' whoever was captain.

As Sellers later admitted, cricket was changing. Unlike Wardle, Illingworth had stuck up for himself, and bettered himself outside Yorkshire. In his 1969 book, *Spinner's Wicket*, he warned that Yorkshire were out of step and risked a 'player-drain':

I still believe there were quite a few of the committee who would have liked me to stay on as a player, but I doubt whether they could have convinced Mr

Sellers. His word seems to be law. Many times he has stated that the club is bigger than the player. I agree with him entirely. I also think, with respect, that the club is bigger than Brian Sellers, which he seems, sometimes to forget.

This neat criticism, picked out in the summer of 1969 in Fleet Street newspapers, of Sellers as over-mighty wounded more than Wardle's ever did, because this came from authority: the new captain of Leicestershire, and England. Yorkshire in 1969 came 13th in the Championship, arguably because Close lacked Illingworth as his deputy. As in all sports, and indeed beyond, Yorkshire was finding that there was more to renewing a team than shedding old players for new.

On Tuesday evening, 24 November 1970 – after Yorkshire had come a creditable fourth in that year's Championship – the club secretary John Nash asked Brian Close to a meeting the next day. 'As I drove the ten miles or so from my home to Headingley I had no idea what the meeting was going to be about,' he said eight years later in his autobiography, the significantly-titled *I Don't Bruise Easily*. 'So it was just a bit of a surprise to find no committee in session, just Mr Nash and Brian Sellers, Mr Yorkshire Cricket.' Sellers said: 'Well, Brian, you have had a good innings.' 'The committee had decided my services were no longer required and that I had to make a decision whether to resign or be sacked.' Close was like the man whose wife tells him she's leaving after 22 years. 'My senses told me that the greatest most overwhelming disaster of my life was taking place yet my mind simply could not grasp the enormity of it all':

I heard myself saying how long have I got to decide because I would like a word with my wife. You have got ten minutes, replied Mr Sellers. The two prepared statements were read over to me and I decided that resignation was the lesser of the two evils. I drove away with my mind in a whirl. I wanted to cry. As I drove along Kirkstall Road my vision misted up so much I had to stop. And then I was sick there at the side of the road.

It was, as Close said, 'the worst day of my life'. Yorkshire had cast him off as suddenly as Wardle, a dozen years before. Close was even more senior than Wardle had been; in his seven years as captain, Yorkshire had been champions four times. Sellers had given it to Close straight; the outcome would not be as straightforward.

The outcomes to this sacking – for the player, and the club - were different from Wardle's, for several reasons.

First, Close did not make Wardle's mistake of giving one exclusive interview. It helped Close's cause that he did not pick a fight – not that the man, first shattered, then mystified, could even think in such deliberate ways. On the regional television news on 2 February 1971 – after the club's annual general meeting – Close denied any vendetta between him and Sellers: 'I have always admired and respected him and I have stuck up for him with the other players.' Yorkshire lacked any logical case; if they blamed Close for shortcomings, why had they kept him – 'a great player', as they admitted?! What reasons Yorkshire did offer, or had twisted by Fleet Street

– such as, Lancashire were more successful at one-day cricket – still did not excuse the way Sellers did it. The *Daily Mirror* for instance deplored the sacking as a slur, by 'a shire where cricketers should be seen and not heard'. What little case the club set out, it made a pig's ear of presenting. The first general committee meeting after the sacking, on 18 December, decided against 'a further statement' and instead settled for a laughably useless 'paragraph' in the annual report, and the offer of an explanation at the AGM; which invited the uproar of 1117 attending on 30 January. By putting members first, worthily enough, the club came across to the wider public, in the media, as unfeeling. The comments of the two main figures in the *Yorkshire Post* after the AGM showed who was on sure ground. Close was already in talks with Somerset, whose captain he became for the next seven seasons:

Mr Sellers said at the annual meeting that my behaviour off the field had on several occasions been far from what it should have been. I am no angel but I have done nothing of which I am ashamed. If they have had complaints on several occasions as they say, I am surprised they have not spoken to me before. I find it strange they should say something now but not when Yorkshire were winning the County Championship or Gillette Cup under my captaincy. They have tried to brand me in public. I want the public to be the jury and if Mr Sellers would meet me say on a TV programme I will be happy to let the public decide. There are several things I could have said over the years but I refrained from doing so because of my love for cricket and Yorkshire in particular. But they started this and I am not going to have the public think I am a rogue.

Sellers, brief and lame by comparison, said the club would hold a special committee meeting: 'I don't know when the meeting will be but we are not going to keep people waiting.' And asked if he would be considering his position, he replied: 'Obviously I will, so will the rest of the committee.'

The press now had a story to follow; the members had revolted, as Wardle had wished for in 1958. At the 1970 AGM, only 111 voted about the South African tour in the apartheid era – a great left-wing cause of the age. Now a majority, 570 to 507, voted against the club report and balance sheet. For hours they debated not only Close (and the choice of Boycott as captain in his place) but the playing strength; why more committee men were from Sheffield than Leeds; even the catering. The leader of an 'action group', Jack Mewies, called the ten minutes given to Close 'disgraceful'. Mewies brought up a letter that Sellers sent to the president of Lancashire, Lionel Lister, after a Sunday match at Manchester in August 1970, when Close had made 'remarks' to Lister. 'Sellers condemned Close without taking his opinion of the incident. This is kangaroo justice,' said Mewies, a solicitor from Skipton.

Richard Ulyatt, writing in the *Yorkshire Post*, felt that in the uproar the committee let the speakers have their say; giving the day to the 'action group' protesters. Sellers did not quite bite his tongue. On the Lister case, which had sounded like two men saying things in the heat of a game best forgotten, Sellers said: 'Knowing Mr Lister I was perfectly certain that what he said was correct. If you lost a game you lost and you have got to accept it. It isn't good talking the way Close did and saying the umpires were bad.' Sellers also said that the committee had wanted to give young players a chance in the Sunday League; Close had not done it. 'There were at least three occasions like that involving young players,' Sellers told the meeting. If the committee were treating Sundays as a time to try out young players, it was hardly taking one-day games seriously – one of the faults they sacked Close for!? Arguably most damaging was what Sellers said in self-defence: 'I am not a dictator. I carry out my duties on the instructions of the committee.' Just as it never sounds good when a husband denies he is a wife-beater, Sellers was admitting that some saw him as a dictator.

Was Sellers lying, or deluded? The minutes of the cricket committee for 1970 back Sellers. Close should have realised he was putting his job in jeopardy. In June, Herbert Sutcliffe asked why the 26-year-old junior batsman John Woodford did not play in a Sunday League match at Hull, as the committee had decided the meeting before. Close admitted to a 'mistake'. In July, when Cope likewise had not played when picked for a Sunday game, Close said he had 'forgotten'. At its 24 September meeting, the committee took Sellers' side over the Lister affair and wrote to Close accordingly. Nor was Close at the next, 22 October meeting ('it was assumed he was away on holiday'). If he imagined he could defy his employer over their selections, he was mistaken. As someone sacked by England over a trifle in 1967, Close should have known better than to give his county excuses to make a fuss. His age, 39, and matches he missed through injuries were already counting against him. After the 1970 season the committee asked two local surgeons to look at Close's arthritic right knee (in 1968, only one looked). The surgeons passed Close fit, with rest, only for the committee at their next meeting on 19 November to doubt it. That, and 'Close's attitude towards one day matches' was enough to do for him. Close was named in the minutes as present at that final meeting; presumably he left when they discussed him. In other years, when that happened, the committee told the captain on his return that they had given him another year. That raises the unpleasant picture of Close sitting in front of men who knew his fate while he did not. Did Close really not pick up something? The committee agreed that Sellers and Nash should 'interview Close as soon as possible and give him the opportunity of resigning'. Sellers was indeed only doing the committee's work.

Members had let off steam at the AGM; they had made newspaper front pages; none of that meant they posed any practical challenge. *The Guardian* reported Sellers saying afterwards: 'All that the rejection of the report means is that the action group have won five points on the first innings. Now it's our turn to bat.' He had a point. The meeting re-elected Sir William Worsley (who had not been at the crucial 19 November meeting), as president; the treasurer and auditor (though the club had shown a loss it admitted was 'disastrous', thanks to the lost South African tour takings); and the vice-presidents, including Sellers. His cricketing metaphor however was telling and unfortunate. He was implying that the protesters were equals; competitors. Just as 'if batsman thinks it's spinnin', it's spinnin'", if some members said the committee was unfit, it was. Later, Kilburn called it 'times of revolutionary disturbances'. In truth the protesters were rebelling; they were not seeking to overthrow those in power. An active handful was making demands that had little to do with the original uproar. The 'action group' asked for contracts for players; vice-presidents 'in honour only' rather than active committee members, postal votes at district elections of committee members, and votes for women. Despite the noise at the AGM, only a fraction of the overall membership had stood out against Sellers. What of the majority; were they loyal to the committee, or plain apathetic?! If the club could no longer count on apathy as permission to do as it pleased, it only had itself to blame for making what the press was already terming a 'controversy' or an 'upheaval'. It had all the ingredients of a running news story: an 'action group' that was keen to put its case across – indeed, too keen, club loyalists complained; and a regular timetable of club meetings, above all that AGM.

In the days after, some journalists took sides – against Sellers, whether on principle or because they were settling scores. Eric Todd in the *Guardian*, below a headline of 'Last innings for Sellers', wrote on 10 February: 'In any democracy there can be no room for the autocrat,' and was surprised that none of the committee had done 'the decent thing and resign'. Kilburn meanwhile suggested in the *Yorkshire Post* that the committee could treat the vote against them as a rebuke, and carry on; yet without the confidence of members, they had no moral right to rule. It left the committee at the mercy of the 'action group'. What would satisfy those complaining? An apology? Better catering?! The very fact that the protesters didn't know what they were doing made it harder for the committee to please them. For instance, Mewies moved a vote of censure and no confidence at the AGM, only to have it ruled out of order, because he hadn't given it in advance.

As in many civil wars, both sides were in the right. Kilburn saw 'the necessity to replace Close', and the action group's 'reasonable quest for reform':

... but I regret their condemnation of Sellers as cricket chairman because I regard it as both uninformed and ill-timed. Sellers and the committee could not defend themselves without making public some factors that might have reflected unfavourably upon a club servant and this as Sir William Worsley explained they were reluctant to do.

Leaving aside that the committee saw its captain not as an employee but a 'servant', the 'action group' did not have to worry about the feelings of others. It got personal – always the easy political choice. After the re-election of Sellers as cricket chairman – his position of power - Jack Mewies told the *Yorkshire Post* on 4 March that he was angry: 'This will annoy thousands of people who made clear their views at the annual meeting.' As only a thousand had attended the AGM, Mewies was only showing himself up as bombastic. 'The re-election of Mr Sellers was the last thing anybody wanted apart from the committee members themselves. It ... seems to show we are wasting our time trying to talk to these people.' Mewies was assuming he was speaking for everybody, and that his unelected 'group' (of how many?!) was on a par with the century-old club. The committee however was so unused to dissent, let alone through the media, that it was leaving the field to Mewies. A fortnight later, the club said that Sellers would retire at the end of the year. This delighted Mewies ('the one really major outstanding point we wanted agreed to'). He wondered aloud why Sellers had not said so sooner.

From the outside, it looked as if Sellers had been holding on to power. The club minutes show how the uproar had undone him months before. At that 24 November general committee meeting, the last one in peacetime, Herbert Sutcliffe gave notice that he would propose Worsley, Sellers and Arthur Mitchell as honorary life members at the AGM. At the next month's meeting, Sellers offered to withdraw his name, 'but following the committee's unanimous insistence he agreed to let his name be put forward'. When Sutcliffe and Yardley publicly proposed and seconded Worsley and Mitchell, Sellers' name had gone. At a meeting on 25 January, when Sellers 'kindly agreed to defend those charges connected with cricket', the general committee was glad to have him. After the AGM, he was not on any of the sub-committees to come up with new rules, or to look into player contracts, finance, or even catering (that his brother Godfrey was a member of). The honorary treasurer, Michael Crawford, not Sellers, met the 'action group'. Sellers had become toxic.

The county claimed that when Sellers, and B.H.Barber, chairman of the finance committee, were re-elected for 1971, they intended the year to be their last; and Sellers had been going to say so, at the usual pre-season lunch on 28 April. The committee had wanted Sellers to stay, rather than have a new captain, and new chairman, in the same year.

Whatever the truth, Yorkshire would be short of experience on and off the field. John Nash was retiring as secretary, aged 65; and Doug Padgett was taking over as coach from the 68-year-old Arthur Mitchell, meaning one fewer old player to aid Boycott. In time for the new season, Sellers, now 64, had resolved Yorkshire's wounds as best he could. 'This has made the way clear for amity,' crowed Mewies; not that the 'action group' was folding. He and his kind must have liked the sound of their own voices, and the sight of their words in print. The next time Yorkshire faltered, every sports journalist knew who to call. Until then, everyone could look forward to some cricket. Geoffrey Boycott was home; he had his left arm in a sling, broken while winning the Ashes in Australia under Ray Illingworth. What else could go wrong?!

Some of those mid-March reports of Sellers' retirement sounded like obituaries. In *The Times*, John Woodcock found it 'hard to believe that he will no longer be heard'. As in obituaries, people offered more sympathy for Sellers, now that he was going. Eric Todd, having come out against Sellers, wrote: 'It would be stupid not to appreciate that according to his own lights, his autocracy was nothing other than discipline which, heaven alone knows' - Todd too was in his 60s - 'is in shorter supply than ever in most walks of life.' Never ones to feel sentimental, the journalists asked who would take over from Sellers. Kilburn in the *Yorkshire Post* doubted Yorkshire would find someone so qualified. Kilburn, always informed, passed judgement not only on a man, but his times, that Kilburn had grown old sharing:

Since 1959 Brian Sellers has given unstintingly of time and service to the promotion of Yorkshire cricket. He has formed judgement on play through innumerable hours of observation and by persistent inquiry. He has advocated the Yorkshire cause at countless meetings and social functions. He has represented the Yorkshire view of cricket at national level and has taken his turn on MCC committees. His personality and passion in cricket has drawn wide publicity on his pronouncements and activities but he has never evaded responsibility nor has he sought personal advantage from the authority of office. He has been forthright in criticism of Yorkshire cricket and cricketers behind closed doors but he has always presented their public defence with unflinching loyalty. He has been a stern leader but never an unjust one and he has borne without rancour much uninformed criticism. By his own choice he would have retired from his present office at least two years ago and he had resolved on yesterday's announcement last autumn before controversy swept into the Yorkshire club. Those who knew him will understand that he is resigning not through opposition to his stay but because he believes he has fulfilled obligations to the limit of his capacity and that change will not harm Yorkshire. He timed his resignation from the captaincy on the same principle.

That's worth quoting so fully, not only because Kilburn would have been Sellers' biographer, but for blindness in old age. Kilburn had revealed something important; that Sellers had resolved on his own retirement, when he gave Close the sack. Sellers may have been tempted into something drastic, when nearing the end of power, as in China Mao Tse-tung had set off the Cultural Revolution. The sacking would wipe the slate clean and give the club a fresh start. A new chairman would be in as powerful a position as could be, with an inexperienced and keen new captain. When Sellers said those few words to Close – 'Well, Brian, you have had a good innings' – Sellers could have been talking to himself.

After a lifetime of upholding the Yorkshire club, at the end did Sellers wish, unconsciously, to bring the house down, Samson-like? For besides the paradox of Sellers as a northerner who served for years on the MCC committee, we have another: Sellers the imposer of authority – 'yes, he was quite imposing,' his son Andrew recalled, 'with his hair parted down the middle; if he wasn't very happy with you, you knew about it' – with an impish, even anarchic streak. Andrew Sellers recalled:

He loved as I did with him on many occasions especially at Sheffield, he would go and sit in amongst the crowd and then he would say some stupid comment about the player or whatever and there would be a hell of a row, an argument starts all the way round which he would get going and then say, 'come on, let's piss off, we have got this lot going', we would leave that lot shouting at each other, then we would go somewhere else and he might do the same thing. That was the sort of thing he liked doing, so we did have a few laughs.

Brian Sellers' brother Godfrey was 'a serious man, and father was the one that created havoc'.

Whatever you think of Boycott's years as Yorkshire captain, and indeed whether you find Boycott interesting or not: that's his story and not Sellers'. We forget easily that the sacking of Close was only half of the equation; the other half was the naming of Boycott. According to Don Wilson, Boycott's first vice-captain, Sellers 'opted for Boycott with his casting vote'. According to the committee minutes, the choice of Boycott (and Wilson) was unanimous. Few minded Boycott at first, partly because no-one could foresee the controversy of the next 15 years, and partly because others too saw him as the likely captain. Illingworth in his 1969 autobiography had named Boycott as Yorkshire captain for the 1970s, over the more senior Phil Sharpe (who led Yorkshire in 1970 when Close was injured). John Hampshire suggested Sharpe or Richard Hutton, 'and my own best bet would have been Duggie Padgett'; except that Hampshire was writing in 1983, and had fallen out, like most, with Boycott. Later still, in old age Sir Leonard Hutton wondered how Boycott would have done under a captain like Sellers. Boycott would not have been the only fish in the pond; and Sellers would have given Boycott 'more explicit instructions', to bat in the way the team wanted, instead of gathering runs at his own speed: 'I believe he would have responded like the rest of us to firm leadership.' The journalist Derek Hodgson, in his history of the club in 1989, offered an intriguing counter-factual: what if Close had given the captaincy to Illingworth in 1972, and Illingworth to Boycott in 1975? However, for that very different Yorkshire history to happen, Yorkshire had to manage its assets differently; it would not have been Yorkshire.

Yorkshire in 1971. Whether the photographer did it on purpose or not, he made the new captain Geoffrey Boycott look bigger than the team.

The sheer inhumanity of the sacking of Close gave Boycott's captaincy a bad start, quite apart from a missing batsman. The sacking put pressure on whoever came next to do better (another reason Sellers did it?). When the county duly finished 13th in the Championship and second from bottom in the Sunday League – and remember Close went because he allegedly did not take one-day cricket seriously enough – it looked as if Yorkshire had made a mistake. Regardless, at the October 1971 committee meeting when he stood down as chairman, Sellers proposed Boycott as captain for 1972 ('carried unanimously'). Sellers had set out his demands at the pre-season lunch in April 1971: 'Our batsmen have to get out there and score more runs and they have got to score them more quickly. Not only that they have got to keep their eyes on the scoreboard. Far too often last year we missed vital bonus points by not even looking at the board.' These were strange words. If the batsmen had been so at fault, why had the captain gone? And if, as their 13th place suggested and as Bill Bowes reported in the 1972 *Wisden*, Yorkshire despite Sellers' words 'did not adjust to the bonus points system', why was the new captain not punished like Close?

It was one more reason why Close's sacking made so little sense outside the committee room. No-one, then or since, has tried to defend the way Sellers did it; not even Sellers. Sir William Worsley, the club president, on television in February 1971 had to admit it had 'probably been handled in the wrong way'. The acting editor of *The Cricketer*, Alan Ross, described it as 'on the face of it ... a clumsy and bungled business'; 'rather odd', Trevor Bailey called it. In his 1987 autobiography Boycott, who had gained from the sacking, ranked it 'as one of the cruellest incidents in the history of sport'. Fred Trueman in old age scorned it as 'another of A.B.Sellers' masterpieces of man-management' and was among the many to repeat a story of Close's. While captain of Somerset Close met Sellers, who confessed that the sacking had proved the worst decision of his life. 'To give him ten minutes, it's awful isn't it,' said Sid Fielden in 2015, after Close's death. 'You hear Closey tell that story, it made you cry. In fact it made Closey cry.'

When something bad happens – a world war, the death of someone in a car accident – we seek reasons, as if reasons make bad things more bearable.

So it is with the sacking of Close, 'the start of something like 30 years of absolute trouble and strife in Yorkshire county cricket,' as Stott put it; with hindsight, as he admitted. What few successes the club could point to – the Second Eleven won the Minor Counties Championship in 1971 – only highlighted what the first team had lost. 'One looks for hidden reasons,' Bill Bowes wrote in the 1972 *Wisden*, without going on to offer any. You only had to read the gospels; a bad tree could not produce good fruit.

Men agreed that Sellers had changed, for the worse. According to John Hampshire, Sellers had gone from 'the Great Democrat' as captain, to the 'Great Autocrat' as chairman: 'You did as he said, or else. And to be painfully frank about it, his thinking was that of an age long since gone by.' As Close and Sellers alike had admitted after the sacking, they had kept their arguments out of the public eye; Close as middle-man between players and committee, as Sellers had been when captain. Ironically, not only in his success, but how he rallied his players, Close 'in many ways was very like Sellers', John Hampshire wrote later.

As Hampshire saw it, Illingworth's move brought about 'the downfall of Yorkshire cricket', as Illingworth - without a formal title, or appreciation by the club - did so much for the team, and for Close. Boycott, like Churchill, has had the knack of writing his own history. His 2014 memoir came with a moving title that spoke of his new perspective on life, as a father, and after recovering from cancer: *The Corridor of Certainty*. Most of the 23 on the general committee were weak and did not want to challenge the cricket committee members, who were mainly former players, he said. 'How do you convince people like Brian Sellers, who had been amateur captain of Yorkshire, that he is wrong?' Sellers, and others, were 'not bad men but they were stuck in their ways, and they did not realise that the game had moved on since their day'. Boycott convinces, yet begs further questions. Why did the club have so many on a committee, that invited long discussions before any decision? Because the club was always a compromise, between the many parts of such a large county, each proud and careful to keep its committee places and fixtures. Put another way, towns and ridings were forever jealous of each other, and above all Leeds. Only such a large committee could satisfy every district. To decide anything - and the club had to keep picking a team, making room for some and disappointing others - the club *needed* an 'autocrat', such as Lord Hawke or Sellers; provided, as in any tyranny, that the man in power was trustworthy. Just as a batsman is only as good as his last innings, so a chairman is only as good as his last decision. Bryan Stott wondered if Sellers received second or third opinions; and if he did, whether he took notice. Sellers is not the first or the last man in power who has made a decision so unwise that it was bad for everyone; even himself. In 1914, the emperors of Germany, Austria and Russia each agreed to a war that left their families deposed or murdered. This is something for humanity to address, if it is serious about surviving as a species.

Steve Troth, a printing apprentice at the Sellers' factory at the time, recalled turning up for work in Bradford after the Close sacking 'to find that every single window in the building had been smashed!'. Sellers' son Andrew recalled Jack Mewies as 'this fool'; 'and idiots from Skipton; we had a rent a crowd bus at the AGM; that basically was the end of father, was that. Times I have been talking to him and all he has been saying, well, it's only a bloody game for Christ's sake; he couldn't understand the way the whole thing had gone around, not against him, but generally against his view of the cricketing world, which eventually I think put him on the road to the end, somehow. He sort of gave up a bit after that. Apart from that, he got the dreadful rheumatoid arthritis so he couldn't do much so it was a bit of a sad end to his career."

Sellers only had to keep his eyes open to see change. A stone's throw from Keighley's cricket club, Holy Trinity Church in Lawkholme Lane, where his parents baptised him in 1907 and where his father had his funeral service, was knocked down in 1972. By sacking Close, Sellers at least showed he was not afraid of change. Sellers however had spent all his credit with the membership by sacking Close. Or rather, Sellers had picked the wrong sort of problem; the challenge for Yorkshire lay not in personnel – one captain or another – but in more profound policy.

As new captain, according to his 1987 autobiography, Boycott felt the squad lacked 'anything like the right blend of talent and experience'. He soon put the point to Sellers that 'Yorkshire needed some new blood, and pretty quickly'. Without spelling it out, Boycott meant, as Sellers would have understood, signings from overseas; that is, men not Yorkshire-born. Boycott added:

I think Sellers agreed but he was not prepared, as chairman of the cricket sub-committee, to invite new controversy by rocking the boat too much. There had been a furore over Close's departure, and Sellers had come in for a lot of personal criticism; I reckon he just wanted a quiet life for what was left of his association with Yorkshire.

Here, beyond the sacking of Close, lay Sellers' ultimate failure. It was nothing new for easy-beat counties to import players and do better; Northamptonshire recruited Freddie Brown as captain, the West Indian Bertie Clarke, and the Yorkshire wicket-keeper Kenneth Fiddling in the 1940s; and Australians in the 1950s. After a new rule in 1968, every county was doing it – except Yorkshire. At Gloucestershire, an all-rounder such as Mike Procter was the equivalent of an extra man. Or – perhaps the most uncomfortable example of all for Yorkshire – a struggling county such as Derbyshire could revive under an inspirational captain such as Eddie Barlow. Even though in the 1960s and 1970s alike Yorkshire had several men good enough to play for England, the county could not hope to keep beating others with world-class foreigners, unless Yorkshire, too, had one or more men of world class. The harder Boycott tried as a batsman to bridge that gap, the less he had to spare as captain; not a burden Sellers had as a player. Sellers was long gone from power by the time the implications unravelled. Whether Boycott heroically kept Yorkshire from even worse failure, or whether he was part of the problem, was beside the point. That is not to say an overseas player or two would have solved Yorkshire's troubles, just as the county's first overseas players did not in the 1990s; many overseas players at many counties did not succeed. Without a 'foreigner', Yorkshire had to be at least as united and excellent as they were in Close's time as captain; and they were not.

Sellers had, as even some of his critics agreed, always done what he thought was best; as a steward of the club. He, like others around him, were true conservatives. Having given a lifetime of service, they took that as their perspective; or even longer, as Sellers had followed his father. These men would not change for the sake of it, or without good reason; they wanted to pass the club on soundly to the next stewards. Such conservatives are valid, even vital to resist the self-seekers, windbags and the money-mad that pass through anywhere. The wisest stewards allow change, even drastic, or too much for some, even many, to bear. A far-sighted Yorkshire clubman in 1970 could have seen it was time to change custom; to recruit an outstanding player from overseas. Garry Sobers, for instance, had played for Yorkshire on tour, and the world had not ended; nor did it when Yorkshire did field its first foreigner, Sachin Tendulkar. Sellers had sailed with the times over professional captains, and one-day cricket; he could have used his clout to make the case for foreigners – or at least tried, as most members were against change. To be a true steward, you have to know what is the essence you are guarding. As a captain, Sellers had seen what was essential easily enough; to beat the other fellows. Stewardship of a club lacked the rules and the win, lose or draw certainty of sport; the opponents off the field had been less obvious than the other eleven men; in the end, Sellers' worst enemy might have been himself. His son Andrew recalled how 'it', the rebellion by members, 'finished him off, just disappointed him so much, he couldn't quite fathom, he couldn't understand what had gone on, he couldn't understand the modern way of thinking or anything like that; there we go.'

Sellers was hardly to blame if those after him were feeble; unless he had not made other strong-minded men welcome, on the Wild West principle of the town not being big enough for the two of them. By the time John Hampshire batted slowly on purpose to miss a bowling point in 1978, a public protest against Boycott that went unpunished, it hardly mattered who was right or wrong any longer. A weak committee was as bad as a failed tyrant.

Chapter Thirteen
Keighley, December 2015

Me, yesterday I was rumour,
today I am legend,
tomorrow, history.
Ian Mudie, They'll Tell You About Me

I came in the dark and left in the dark. I stepped off the train at Keighley and walked the rising path to the street. Before a long day in the town library I wanted something to eat and something to read with it. I bought a *Yorkshire Post* from the station kiosk, and in the café on the corner ordered eggs and chips. As the day dawned grey I read about Joe Root's autobiography. They were sock-snipping in the England dressing room now.

Sock-snipping!

I was no longer sitting in Keighley in 2015; that word took me back to the basement canteen of the *Evening Press* in York in 1995 when I was the sports editor of the *Yorkshire Gazette & Herald*. Someone had shown me the internet recently, and I could not see it catching on. I read in the *Yorkshire Post*, or the *Northern Echo*, of the then Yorkshire captain David Byas annoyed by a phantom sock-snipper in his dressing room. Why did that, of all things, stick in my head? Because, 20 years later, I would find a use for it? Because of the mystery? Because ruining socks by cutting through them at the heel so offended me? Or because the story gave a rare insight into the true nature of sportsmen, ordinary and even childish?

The sock-cutting was happening to the same group of men as Sellers' – though the personnel had changed a dozen times or more – perhaps even in the same rooms. It's hard to imagine – and shows the change in outlook, still within living memory – anyone daring to snip Sellers' socks, or anyone else's. Men had more respect for socks in Sellers' day. Money was short enough for most so that when your sock wore thin, you (or more likely your wife or mother) would darn it. To damage a sock, you would have to rise above the taboos against waste and respect for other people's property. Even then, to play a prank upon anyone in the dressing room, let alone the skipper, suggested that you had time to spare; not only to do the snipping, but to watch for the moment the room was empty. Under Sellers, you never had that time; as Ted Lester recalled: 'When Yorkshire were batting all the other members of the team were compelled to watch and nobody could disagree with the Sellers argument that only by watching could you learn about the strengths and weaknesses of the opposition.' Lester shuddered to think what Sellers would have done to players sunbathing, or watching television and not the match.

Teams of the past, that we see in sepia photographs with set faces, look more solemn; they were not. Practical jokes were always a part of cricket, Hammond wrote, 'but the good captain must see that they are kept within reasonable bounds'. Sellers' teams welcomed a joke, precisely because they were always busy; fielding, batting, watching others bat, the opponents bowl; signing autographs. If Sellers' men had any spare time or energy, they had to put it towards a purpose; of becoming better cricketers, or simply to remain useful enough to the team. What a contrast with the sock-snipper in Byas' time, who had too much imagination; maybe a grudge, or thwarted ambition. The snipping plainly riled Byas, and with reason, for it undermined his authority. The snipper was mocking the skipper.

Sock-snipping has become a part of modern English cricket folklore; a tradition to keep up, even. It must answer a psychological need in some; or, it binds a group. To have cut Sellers' socks would have simply been beyond the mind of his players. We can no more imagine it than we can imagine Bill Bowes with his hair dyed red, or Maurice Leyland rapping.

*

Nothing really changed after Sellers retired as chairman, said Boycott; Sellers stayed on the general committee, 'where he was able to still rule the club with an iron fist'. Yorkshire had the worst of all worlds; the old tyrant was out of office, and the new chairman was John Temple, a committee man from York since 1956, 'a weak, malleable man' according to Boycott. As captain, Boycott was a witness; yet Geoff Cope showed more practically the difference in regimes. In 1970 Cope was 'on trial' at Lord's, as the newspapers put it, for a suspicious bowling action. When 'this problem' began, as Cope called it in later life, Sellers was 'very supportive':

He was a man of colourful language and suggested that I put my backside on Pudsey station at such and such a time to get the morning train. And he got on at Bradford, I got on at Pudsey and with him was Arthur Mitchell, who was then the coach, Ticker Mitchell. And if I say I got good morning, sit there, and the next time we spoke we were in London; but in between he and Arthur had talked about the game of cricket and it was probably one of the finest educations that I had had, just listening to these two reminiscing, bringing the modern game in, as it was in those days, and saying how things had changed.

We got down there and he spoke up on my behalf and I was very grateful to him for his support.

Andrew Sellers added how his father 'spoke up': '... so father said, come on Geoff, we will wait until they get a decent committee together, then we will come back, let us know when you have got a mixed committee, you are all southerners, and we are not listening to it. They came back on the train.' Cope recalled that his bowling action came up again, under the new chairman, 'and I said, oh, when do we go to Lord's? The answer was, oh, we don't go to Lord's; and the answer there was clearly Brian was going against the establishment.' While Cope was not close to him, Sellers had stuck up for the young player; 'and I shall never, ever forget that'.

The words men used to describe Sellers, alive or dead, were of a kind. Formidable, said many, including Sir Len Hutton. Forceful, said Trevor Bailey. Sellers was 'most forthright' (Hutton again); 'a colourful character' (Cope and others); 'lively', said Yardley in a 1962 newspaper column. 'Dominating personality', wrote Swanton. All these are revealingly imprecise. They leave it to us to imagine what sort of force or domination; for good or bad? Yardley's memoir is useful, for its date – when Sellers was at his cricketing crossroads, turning from captain to committee man – and because Yardley, as one of the few men who could hold his own against Sellers socially and in playing ability, simply dared to write at length:

Sellers is not a martinet, but he is a disciplinarian almost in the Lord Hawke tradition. Yet he has an unsurpassed sense of humour. He is fearless in making decisions, fearless against any bowling in any situation, and equally fearless in Committee where he speaks his mind without reserve, and where his vivid personality is respected by everyone.

Lord Hawke approved of what he saw; 'the right type of leader', he called Sellers at Yorkshire's annual meeting in 1933. 'That most adept captain', the *Times* called him in its preview of the 1948 season; by 1938, 'unquestionably the best captain in the world', wrote Bill Bowes. Ian Peebles (one of Sellers' few first-class bowling victims) called him able, courageous and thrusting; the *Daily Worker*, in its 1948 cricket handbook, able and outspoken. By 1948, Hammond had cause to hate or ignore Sellers; instead he was warmer than many:

... one of the finest models any young cricket captain could wish; he was a great-hearted fighter, a most dogged batsman, and one who kept his team of 'Tykes' perfectly in hand with a wonderful mixture of jokes and discipline that they all loved.

Everyone was defining Sellers; and while you will always find differences (he *was* at times a martinet, according to Bowes), a pattern emerges, in what people said and did not. Few said what *they* thought of him. Because they did not dare; because it was better unsaid? Besides asking those that knew him best, we should also look to outsiders, less used to him. Some found Sellers hurtfully blunt or foul-mouthed. In September 1951, the 18-year-old Colin Cowdrey made 106 for the Gentlemen against the Players at Scarborough, the highest score of the match. Cowdrey was not playing in the last match of the festival, and as he was leaving the Grand Hotel, he had 'an encounter':

I said, 'Goodbye Mr Sellars,' [sic] to which he replied, 'Judging by the shot you got out to I'm not surprised that you are not playing in the last match up here.'

I was thunderstruck. What I did not know at that shattering moment, was that this was Sellars' manner with everyone. I was going out of the door when his voice boomed again, 'Hey, coom back, coom back. Listen lad, I want to tell you something. If you're not playing for England and on the boat to Australia there'll be only one person to blame. You'll be to blame. It'll be your fault and nobody else's.' I was many miles down the A1 before I realised this was a back-handed compliment.

We know Cowdrey was on the threshold of a long and fine career; he did not, and Cowdrey was evidently unsure enough of himself to dwell on Sellers' 'shattering' opinion. Did Sellers, the man of dramatic entries, also enjoy the impression he made on the young and well-spoken? Another Oxbridge man and future England captain, Tony Lewis, recalled in his 2003 memoir the shock of his first handshake with Sellers, and his words: 'Na then, you little Welsh bastard.' As with Australians, 'bastards' was not meant nastily. In his earlier, 1985 memoir Lewis recalled Sellers, 'of the severe countenance and intimidating reputation' usually greeting Lewis to Scarborough with: 'Na then y'Welsh bastard. What do you make of this bluddy lot then?'

Sellers made a habit of it. Brian Dolphin of Sutton-in-Craven recalled Sellers captained a team in an invitation match at Beckwithshaw near Harrogate around 1960. The Bedser twins were umpires. Sellers 'was sat on a seat with some ladies' when the Bedsers arrived 'and Brian said, 'now then you Surrey b****s. How are you?" And when Sellers had run out one of his own players, Sellers told him: 'You run as if you have a bat up your arse!' As Brian Dolphin added: 'He could be quite crude!'

As elsewhere with Sellers, some skirted over his swearing. Hutton for instance in old age called it 'straight talking'. Bryan Stott recalled that Sellers would swear at dinners, 'even if the bishop was there', or ladies: 'If he was giving grace, I won't tell you what he used to say for grace, it was unnecessary.' Though most would not embarrass themselves by repeating Sellers' swear-words, we need to confront it. This very hiding of a part of Sellers should make us more curious.

We should also confront our own prejudices, and not assume that only the working-class swear, because common people are coarse; when in fact some common people do not swear and do not like to hear it, and our supposed betters, leaders in politics and business, and the most sensitive artists, can and do swear. Otherwise Sellers – as one of cricket's elite, privately-educated, who yet spoke with a northern accent and swore so readily – will confuse us.

Some swear because their work is harsh; soldiers, sailors, the police, miners, labourers and criminals. Cricketers, who played to win, had to live with defeat - perhaps often - and face their own failure. Swearing might serve as an accepted way of releasing personal and group pain, even by those who would not swear otherwise. Dickie Bird said 'language' (another word to hide swearing) 'couldn't be worse than that used in the Yorkshire team in my early days', in the late 1950s. Players by swearing acknowledged the violence of sporting competition, team against team and by every man for a place in a team. By swearing, men shared a culture;

and as in any group, by swearing they were as much keeping others out, if they conformed to society by speaking politely outside the dressing room and in print. Just as Freemasonry insists on keeping its words and phrases to itself, so swearing was a secret among sportsmen.

That can explain Sellers' swearing when playing. What was his excuse as the committee chairman? Trueman was perceptive: "He would curse and swear like a trooper, and you could believe, if you were terribly misguided, that he was 'one of the boys'." Whether by Trueman's time Sellers swore out of habit, or by choice, swear words coarsened conversation; by forcing the hearer to listen, Sellers was making everyone else accept his right to swear at them. As Illingworth told it, after he sent in his letter of resignation, Bill Bowes told him that Sellers had said Illingworth could go, 'and any bugger else that wants to can go with you'. In an age, tellingly, of ever more freedom to swear – or put another way, those that like to swear are forcing the rest of us to live with it – we might not be able to judge how bad a swear-word 'bugger' was in Yorkshire in 1968. As always, it depended on time and place and audience. While according to Boycott, in this case Sellers said 'fuck' rather than 'bugger', both could be right; Sellers might have used either in different conversations. If Bowes or Illingworth had swapped the then unprintable 'fuck' for the more tolerable and, in Yorkshire, even endearing 'bugger', we can see that like any taboo, swearing required the victim to share the guilt of the secret. As in sexual abuse, that the innocent could not easily admit that they were sworn at was part of the hold that the swearer had over them.

The players could not swear back. Sellers 'called spades bloody shovels', John Hampshire recalled: 'His language was that of a navvy to his workmate, labouring on a building site, but his attitude was that of the NCO to the humblest private.' In that one sentence, Hampshire pointed at how professional sport was an occupation like any other; and its connection with the military. Swearing came easily; it could put a man down; it was a sign of harsh man-management - 'hardly a silken art form in Yorkshire', Boycott recalled later. To swear at a man denied him compassion. However, in professional sport, that did serve a purpose. As Basil D'Oliveria said - a useful 1960s source as an incomer to English cricket – 'nice chaps win nothing'. Here was a social paradox; Yorkshire were as D'Oliveria saw 'the aristocrats of the game'. They would do anything to win, short of cheating. Being brutish rather than 'nice' was a choice; a necessary hallmark of winners, even. Stuart Surridge, Surrey's winning captain of the 1950s, said that he learned this lesson from Sellers: 'He told me you get nothing for coming second.'

Willie Watson, who gave more of his autobiography over to Sellers than most, did not say Sellers swore, while making plain that Sellers meant his words to hurt: 'If you received the lash of the skipper's tongue on the field you felt about the size of a midget.' Despite summing up Sellers – twice – with a cliché, 'strict disciplinarian' (is there any other sort?!), Watson did get across how everything Sellers did was for a purpose:

Off the field he was a cheerful character who liked a joke and who liked a drink with the boys. In fact, he liked anything that helped towards making the Yorkshire team the happiest, smartest and most efficient in county cricket. He disliked everything that would interfere with that ambition.

Wardle, who also in print called Sellers a 'strict disciplinarian', found Sellers a just man: 'He played (and let everyone know he played) that the game is more than the player and the ship is more than the crew.' If Sellers' ambition was Yorkshire's, did every player's well-being fit with it? Not always.

Here then is a truth about team sport, and any group; the interests of the institution do not match those of the individual, no matter what anyone says to kid themselves or others. It took a captain, Ron Burnet, to give the crucial insight. In a book of tributes to Hutton he was one of the few to say what one man made of another. 'Len certainly got on all right with Norman [Yardley] – whether he always got on with Brian Sellers I wouldn't really know. I don't think anybody really, really got on with Sellers.' Was it coincidence that Sellers was the most successful county captain of all time, and Yardley only shared one Championship? Did getting on with your fellow players get in the way of winning?

Just as a general has to harden himself to order men into battle, where some will die, so the cricket captain cannot allow himself to feel too warm towards any player, that he may have to order to do something not in his best interests – bat recklessly to make quick runs so that the team can declare; or stand down for a younger man, who will take his place for good if he does well enough. The leader – captain or committee chairman – sometimes has to tell an untruth to motivate. Ted Lester as second team captain understood this on Thursday 20 August 1959, at Bridlington. On the second day of two, having made Lincolnshire follow on, only two wickets had fallen by tea.

As I walked off the field the chairman collared me and said when you get back to the dressing room I want you to tell those lazy so and sos that this just won't do. If there isn't a vast improvement after tea I will be looking for some new players. Now go and get a cup of tea and do what I say. Just before we went back on to the field I simply said to the players the chairman is not very satisfied with our performance this afternoon so let's go out and really show him what we can do.

The seconds took the last wickets and left themselves three overs to make 29; they finished one short. As they sat disappointed in the dressing room there was a knock on the door: 'Well done boys. That was an excellent performance,' Sellers said. 'Now when you have got changed if you will come into the bar I will buy you all a drink.' Sellers did, 'and as he and I were having a quiet conversation', Lester recalled 40 years later, 'he said something which I can never forget':

You know they weren't doing too badly this afternoon when I arrived but it never does any good to let them know that. Far better to express dissatisfaction with a view to getting a bit out of them and if you can get a little bit extra out of everyone it can mean the difference between winning and losing. As I remembered the times he had subjected us to this treatment I could only think, you crafty devil.

Bowes was right; Sellers was only interested in performances. Kilburn, as early as 1950, saw it all:

Sometimes the players thought he was carrying determination beyond the point of reason, sometimes his discipline was considered harsh and sometimes he was less than tactful, but his mistakes were those of a man with the strongest sense of duty conscious of carrying a responsibility beyond personal considerations. He neither courted favour nor feared unpopularity and he never shirked a task, however distasteful, which he regarded as part of the duty of his office.

The crucial words here are 'responsibility' and above all 'duty'; to a cause, a thing, the Yorkshire club, that Sellers felt he had to work to, regardless of men; even – and this would have helped Sellers win his team over – himself. When two batsmen find that either of them could be run out, you can see where power lies; who chooses, or refuses, to be run out. Tellingly, Sellers did not insist that players respect his rank. In June 1937 at Headingley, Sellers was run out when Turner sent him back, 'when Sellers ill-advisedly started for a run for a shot by Turner'. As the batsman more set, and one higher than him in the batting order, Turner was more important to the team than Sellers; Turner did not feel obliged to suffer for Sellers' error.

How did Sellers view his players, whether as captain or chairman? According to Don Mosey Sellers' outlook was feudal, 'more feudal than any venerable MCC Committeeman at Lord's' (which forgot that Sellers did indeed put in years at Marylebone). Sellers was like a 'medieval condottiere to his mercenaries'; or 'like a medieval baron exercising feudal rights'. Mosey did not get his history right; mercenaries notoriously took money and avoided fighting. Mosey had a point; he was suggesting that Sellers demanded – and got – something more than the industrial routine, of work in return for a wage; something aggressive, almost military, based on those intangibles of loyalty to a man, when captain; and duty to an institution, when chairman. Sellers sailed with good humour through the clashes over manners that can arise on any field of play. E.M.Wellings, a fellow journalist on the 1946/47 tour of Australia, recalled a match between the Australian and English press and a school; when an unnamed pompous pressman was disgusted that the agency reporter Norman Preston wore a wrist watch on the field, Sellers prompted the ten fielders to wear their watches. 'I was one 'old cock sparrer' who had plenty of time for Brian Sellers,' Wellings reminisced. That probably said as much about Wellings – a stickler for standards, and not shy to say so – as Sellers.

With his love of gesture and strong opinion, Sellers ought to run through players' memoirs of the 1930s to the 1960s like a stick of rock. Where he doesn't, it's telling. Hutton lay depressed in a Wakefield hospital bed in 1941, wondering if he would ever play cricket again after breaking his arm; in his mind's eye he saw his 'chums in the Yorkshire team'; Mitchell, Barber, Sutcliffe, Leyland, Wood, Verity and Bowes; a long list, but no

*Sellers joined in the social side of an MCC tour –
and the mixing of Australian and English journalists, who formed a team.
Left to right: Vic Richardson, Clarrie Grimmett, Vivian Jenkins, Arthur Mailey,
Bill O'Reilly, George Duckworth, Brian Sellers, Percy Beames, Bill Bowes,
Jack Fingleton. Note the two Australians' wrist-watches in sight.*

Sellers.

In his 1978 and 2013 memoirs, Dickie Bird told the story slightly differently of how Sellers gave him the news he would play in the seconds, even after carrying his bat for 181 for the first team. Only in the 2013 book did Bird write of calling out to Sellers, as he turned to walk away: 'Mr Sellers, I'm so proud to be part of a great Yorkshire squad':

He didn't know what to say. It was true. I was proud. Still am. But I was a little bit hurt by the chairman's attitude. And the resentment began to grow … I was playing the best cricket of my life, yet they kept leaving me out of the first XI.

Bird ended the 1959 season left out of Yorkshire's final match against the Rest, though happy after Sellers told him he would 'definitely' play the next season. Instead, Ron Burnet was sacked, Vic Wilson became captain, and at the start of the 1960 season, and the southern tour, 'Sellers read the names out in alphabetical order. I wasn't in the Bs, perhaps he'd got it in lower down. But he hadn't. I wasn't in. I cried.' Bird went to Leicestershire instead; and his playing career petered out. Bird had reason to resent Sellers, if Sellers said one thing in 1959 and did another in 1960. Yet Sellers could only have picked Bird by leaving someone else out, who then might have resented it. Any leader that hired and unhired would cause as much upset as happiness. A player cast out of the team, or not let in at all, might blame himself for not being good enough. Just as above the gate at Auschwitz the Nazis placed a sign, 'Jedem das seine', 'everyone gets what he deserves', so Bird and almost every player at some stage would feel the same; if he hadn't had enough chances to succeed, he had to accept it was on merit, otherwise the whole system was in the wrong. Why then accept the tyrant, with power to ruin your career? Because, although we are not supposed to admit it, because we so pride ourselves on our democracy, in a country where a good many of us never vote: we *like* rule by a tyrant, because it saves us from hard choices. From having to bother.

*

Not that tyranny is best; not necessarily. The Yorkshire committee not only got its own way, but presented the face it wanted to the world; the one that made it look good, naturally. Hence it insisted in November 1959 on Burnet's 'retirement'. In a letter to John Nash the club secretary, released to the press, Burnet wrote he had 'discussed' with 'Mr Sellers', 'and I was willing, if required, to do another year, but have decided that as the team is now on the right lines and bearing in mind my own limitations as a first-class cricketer, it would best serve the interests of Yorkshire cricket if I retired and made way for a younger man.' In truth Burnet did not want to go and Sellers made him, and Burnet agreed not to rock the boat; to take another comparison from a 20th century tyranny, Stalin had Russian Communist leaders arrested and shot, who as a last service to the Party agreed to pretend they were spies and wreckers. Sellers, like Stalin, needless to say, never had to go through his own treatment; Sellers stood down from the county committee only in 1980, the last full year of his life. Few players were as wise as Bryan Stott and Fred Trueman, and gave up while they could still choose. In his memoirs, Trueman recalled how in 1968 he handed his letter to the president, Sir William Worsley, then drove to see Sellers.

I gave Brian Sellars [sic] my letter. He invited me to sit down and poured us a drink. At one point during our conversation Brian said something that puzzled me. He told me that, inadvertently, perhaps, I had helped the Yorkshire committee out of a difficult situation.

Trueman wondered if the club was planning to sack Close, and offer him the captaincy. 'But we are talking here of the Yorkshire committee, a body of people not exactly known to display loyalty to players, an administration not known for always making the right decisions.'

Like politicians, who will speak well (or not at all) of rivals and enemies when they are dead, Sellers did at least have a habit of giving tributes to retiring players. Sellers said of Trueman: 'Although it is with very great regret that we part with him, I am sure that in his own interests he has done the right thing.' These were the same two men who, as Fred Trueman recalled in old age, had 'some monumental clashes'. After Taunton in 1962 – when Trueman could easily have gone, had he not held his temper – the 'worst insult of the lot' came on Saturday 31 July 1965, when Trueman did not try hard enough to field the ball once in a Roses match, while still trying to put his sweater on after bowling. As his autobiography *Ball of Fire* in 1976 put it:

When I got back to the dressing room Brian Sellers was waiting for me, clearly an angry man. He accused me of not trying, which was ridiculous after I had bowled myself silly to get six wickets [actually five]. *And then he called me a bastard in front of everybody. Now I had learned to keep my temper, but sitting there in the dressing room was my elder brother Arthur, a big, proud man. The chairman was the luckiest man in the whole of Yorkshire that day because Arthur is a hard man and very strong from working in the pit and proud of his younger brother, and it would not have surprised me if he had struck him there and then. I managed to smooth things over. If he had said that a few years before I would probably have thumped him myself, but by then I was the senior professional and had to try to set an example.*

We can query this story of Trueman's, like others of his. Would Arthur Trueman, miner, really have punched Brian Sellers while a guest, knowing he would land his famous brother in trouble? That Arthur Trueman, an outsider, took offence is significant. Had the players become so used to Sellers' 'discipline' (a codeword for making workers obey without ever asking their point of view) that they were bullied? Not if by bully we mean the boy at school who thumped you unless you gave him your dinner money. At least you and he were equals; often you find the bully is himself bullied, by teachers, or family. We ought instead to compare Sellers with the prefect or teacher who lorded it over the less powerful. On 12 August, the committee suspended Trueman for one match, for 'reluctance to obey the captain's instructions on the field'. Any repeat would mean 'instant dismissal'. That news led the next day's front page of the *Yorkshire Post*. Sellers sounded as harsh in print as he did in committee: 'All Trueman has to do is trip over a match and he is finished.'

At least Sellers was consistent. In July 1952, when Trueman took eight for 31 for England against India at Manchester, he left the field to shower and change his shirt, knowing Hutton would enforce the follow-on. Two weeks later during the Roses match, Sellers confronted Trueman in the toilets. 'I've been wantin' to have a word with thee. Just who the hell do you think you are, walking off the field first at Old Trafford?' Trueman explained. 'I don't give a bugger about that. In future, wait until you are asked to go off the field first.'

A generation later, as Cope recalled, Sellers would walk the length of the Old Trafford pavilion, 'knock on our door in the dressing room and say, may I use your toilet; well, he didn't quite say that; but you have got to imagine what he said' – again, that strange unwillingness to give the secrets of swearing in the dressing room – 'and he used the back of our areas.'

Sellers evidently found it hard to give up the players' physical space – even

Rustlewood, above Bingley, the Sellers' 1950s home.

the most intimate. Sportsmen, understandably, do not want to admit they are too old to belong any longer; nor do they like to stop earning a living. What made it worse – in Sellers' time, and after - was that so many mistook the Yorkshire club for something more than a place of work. Wardle admitted in his final article in 1958, 'for a proud Yorkshireman to leave Yorkshire is a big wrench'. Close said on television in 1971: 'If I am guilty of anything it is probably that I was too fervent.' Geoff Boycott, sacked as Yorkshire captain in 1978, said at the end of *Put to the Test,* his book on the 1978/79 tour of Australia: 'Yorkshire is an emotional thing for me.' All three cared too much about an institution that *could not* care for them back. During the Wardle affair, before Wardle's three newspaper articles, Swanton wrote: 'If a family do not get along it is better for them to agree to differ than to nag at one another under the same roof.' While Swanton was right enough, a county cricket club is not a family. For the players, it is their employer, like a factory, or the pit. In their confusion, the players were asking for trouble. In Sellers, Wardle and Close found a chairman hard enough to give them that trouble. The committees after Sellers, in their weakness, merely spun out the trouble for Boycott, and themselves.

*

Sellers and Bright began married life in a Bingley cul-de-sac, Langley Avenue. By 1948, when the Yorkshire club annual listed him as a committee member for Bradford, they lived five minutes' walk away, at Rustlewood, Parkside. Then as now it stands on the right as you climb the valley out of town. Over the road are woods, good for Sellers to walk the dog. From

1966 he lived at Heather Bank, ten minutes' walk away, in the village of Eldwick. Then as now it was on the edge where man's building ended and nature began. Little if any traffic passes and you can hear birdsong and the rush of a stream, out of sight down deep banks. It is a place of drystone walls; somewhere to retreat to. By 1978 he was living at 34 Southway in Eldwick, a bungalow about halfway between his previous two homes, on a somewhat windswept height, with a more distant view of the moors. The front and back gardens were small, far smaller than Heather Bank's. It was a place for an old man to live quietly in, until he was dead.

In his obituary of Sellers in February 1981, Kilburn called the captain 'forthright' (again) 'and devoted in obligation to duty'. John Arlott in the *Guardian* captured the essence of the captain and committee man.

Tall, strong-necked, high-shouldered – and he generally hunched them hostilely higher than they really were – fit and alert, he led his team with unfailingly truculent purpose; though he had a sharp sense of humour. He brooked neither slackness nor argument in his players – his discipline was questioned only at the cost of dismissal – but he would have gone to the scaffold in support of their loyal effort. He learnt much of strategy from the many shrewd cricketers who served under him: but if he erred, they would support him, or he would know the reason why.

After playing, Sellers according to Arlott was 'characteristically inflexible, putting county loyalty and discipline above all other considerations. He was not always sympathetic, nor imaginative; he could be savagely intolerant.' Hardly a personality to want to remember. 'He never, though, wavered from his belief in the traditional values of cricket as played and administered in Yorkshire since the last century.' While more creditable, that left Sellers in the past. Another reason why Sellers' name has not lasted well is that Arlott judged Sellers 'not worth his place as a player ... but there can be no doubt that his captaincy added immensely to the county's strength'. The service of any amateur captain, and the service given to him by the professional players, have gone right out of fashion in a society that prizes the professions – and whose qualified members are so keen to keep it that way. Professional sports teams have so many coaches now, a club can pick the captain out of the eleven and get by. In any case the work of a captain has always been less visible than the six-hits of a batsman or the fast bowler who makes stumps fly. Besides, the break between the old and the new since the 1960s has uprooted cricket from its past. The young have nothing to learn from the old; hence the fall in interest in cricket's past; and if it wasn't televised, you can hardly prove that it happened. Perhaps the cricketers of the 21st century, who shower and drive away as soon as they can after play, are right. To them it is only a job; those clashes between players and Sellers, each side caring so much about *their* club, make no sense in an age when few players stay anywhere more than a few seasons. The counties have become so even, it's hard to see anyone ever matching the record of Sellers, or Surridge or Close. If anyone looks that good, they move for more money, and chances are that England will take them, and their county will never see them until

Heatherbank, on the edge of the moors at Eldwick outside Bingley, the Sellers' later 1960s home.

their thirties, and by then few feel like giving more years to 'their' county. So much of the world as in Sellers' head has gone; cricket and otherwise.

The men of Sellers' time have gone too, or grown old. Now it is too late, they understand that it is wrong to put your faith in one man, if it means you are blind to the point of view of another; or to love one group, if it means you hate another. In short, they learned compassion, for others and themselves.

Geoff Cope asked Sellers to speak at a dinner for his benefit.

I met him at the stairs and I gave him one of the benefit ties and he looked at me and there was a filling up in the eyes, and he said, get on with you, and he sent me packing, and then he saw me later and said, now you never tell anybody you saw me like that; but nobody has ever given me a tie before. That's a soft emotional side of what is described as a very hard man.

As Cope's benefit year was 1980, perhaps Sellers only felt such sentiment, or only let it show, at the very end of his life.

Who are we to judge? Even towards the end, Sellers felt he had to keep up his reputation. As what? A man given power, who used it. What else was he supposed to do with it? Sellers hurt others and made mistakes; who has not? Most of us have not known what it is like to be in power – often because, in so many clubs, and democracies, most members and citizens don't want the trouble. If anyone judges him, it should be the players. Sellers, though blinkered, was 'Yorkshire through and through', as Bryan Stott put it. 'If only men like him would use their power with more discretion, advising instead of trying to dictate,' Trueman said in *Ball of Fire*

Sellers' final home at Southway, Eldwick.

in 1976, when it was too late for everyone. As revealing were Trueman's brave words in 1961; brave, because they came out while Sellers ruled: 'Unlike some of the blokes I have never been scared by Mr Sellers because I know him to be straightforward and sincere in everything he does. He might give you a reight rollocking but he will finish by shaking hands – there is no malice borne – and you can go off and sup a gill together as if nothing has been said.' Let us leave them there.

*

We leave them there; that is not quite where we end. In his great poem in memory of Yeats, Auden wrote that Yeats 'became his admirers'. What did Sellers become? Most of us after our physical death live on in our children; in stories told; and in such intangible things as the example we set, and our reputation. As MCC head coach in the 1980s, Don Wilson insisted on a dress code of blazer and tie, 'even on the hottest days'; a legacy of Sellers, who had insisted on the same of his players at the lunch table. Perhaps while Andrew Sellers lives, Brian Sellers does not die: 'Where he went he liked to make a stir, I have got a bit of that character; I like to get things going, be rude to everybody, sort of take what I am given and give back, to which everybody says, oh, you are just like your bloody father.'

Andrew Sellers in old age was still hearing stories from strangers: 'I don't know half the stuff that went on. When he was at home he was a family man and he wasn't a great lover of the press of course. He kept the family side – we very rarely, apart from various cricketers coming to stay or have meals with us, we really would not have known that cricket was involved, which is the way he wanted it, and that was the way it was.' Many have never heard of Brian Sellers, 'but that would not have bothered him in the slightest'. Such indifference to others might also explain why he left instructions for his body to go to Leeds Medical School, 'because he didn't want any funeral. Because he said, I have been to lots of other people's funerals and got fairly well pissed; well, none of the buggers are going to mine. My brother and I got into a bit of an argument about that with various people, who rang up and said well, there should be a funeral of some description.' Sellers and his wife had a memorial service at Bingley in 1983, which Sellers had not wanted either: 'He didn't want anything. He just wanted to quietly disappear.'

In 1999, Sellers' memorabilia went to auction at Ilkley. A silver salver signed by the 1932 Championship team went for £1150. A smaller silver salver from 1935 (perhaps smaller because by then the buyers realised this man could win many more Championships, and put them to much more expense) went for £360. Sellers became whoever bid most for him.

Not everything went to auction. Geoff Cope said in 2016:

I look across at my little trophy cabinet and amongst all my other things, all Yorkshire caps, England caps, there's actually a ball that Andrew Sellers gave me. Andrew and David, his two sons, because they knew what I thought of Sellers ... it's now so worn it's very difficult to see; a time he took five catches in an innings against Essex; and they have given me that ball that's mounted with a silver wrap around it; and it stands with the rest; I am very proud of that.

Burton upon Trent, December 2015- 9 April 2016

Thanks and sources

Before I came this far, I thought I would enjoy this part the most; instead I have felt the numb sadness at the end of a journey in good company. It began, I know now, on Friday 27 January 2012, in the centre of Manchester. I finished a job by mid-afternoon and on my way to Piccadilly station stopped at the second-hand book stall on the corner by the Arndale shopping centre. I was rummaging in a cardboard box of papers about cricket and came upon several sheets of handwriting on lined A4 paper. The words were of someone in conversation; it had nothing to identify who was speaking or writing the words. I had to rescue it. I was careful to choose a few books too, so that the stall-holder did not see how precious the papers were to me. I forget how much I paid; about £10 the lot.

Some of the interview, which ran to 2000 words, went in my history of English cricket, *The Summer Field*. Once I had given myself a rest after writing that, I began on Brian Sellers; because the man speaking could only be him. The interview seemed to date after Illingworth left the club, and before the row over Close going: between summer 1968 and autumn 1970. Who took down the words; and why were they (and no others) in a cardboard box? I should have bought the whole box; I could have carried it; I have been back since, but it was no longer there. I assumed the interview was genuine, if only because: why would someone forge it, and leave it in a cardboard box?! I got it into my head that the former Fleet Street sports reporter, and historian of the Yorkshire club, Derek Hodgson, had done the interview. I met his son Myles at the 2015 annual conference of the British Society of Sports History (BSSH), who passed me on to his father, who told me he was not the interviewer. The only likely interview I have found was by Richard Dodd in the *Yorkshire Post* on 4 February 1969, which like the anonymous one ranged over Sellers' playing years and the present, although some of the interview in print was not in the longer handwritten one.

Through Martin Howe, the biographer of Norman Yardley, I wrote to and spoke to Sidney Fielden, who gave me the idea of speaking to Geoff Cope. I am grateful to the Yorkshire club for passing my letter on to Cope, secretary of the Yorkshire former players' association.

It turns out that I have been gathering material for this work for five decades, without knowing it, as the first England tour I followed was of Australia in 1978/79, and one of the first cricket books I read was Geoff Boycott's *Put to the Test*.

For Sellers' family background and early life I looked at Keighley newspapers upstairs in Keighley's fine Carnegie library; and the *Telegraph & Argus*, in Bradford library. I learned useful background about the Yorkshire club in the 19th century from a talk at that BSSH conference by Jeremy Lonsdale.

For Sellers' years as captain: the *Yorkshire Post* in Leeds central library, and the *Sheffield Daily Telegraph* in Sheffield central library. For the *Yorkshire Evening Post*: Doncaster library. The *Newcastle Morning Herald* (in Australia) also carried Sellers' 1946/47 Test reports, which you can read online at trove.nla.gov.au. Just as for my *Victory* book I enjoyed hunting newspaper reports in the towns the Australians played in, so I followed Sellers' team around the country to read old evening newspapers: at The Hive, Worcester; Oxfordshire History Centre, Oxford; Cambridge central library; Nottingham central library; Derby local studies library, and the Magic Attic, Swadlincote; Birmingham central library; Leicestershire record office; and Northampton library. For London evening, and national 'papers, I used the British Library at St Pancras; the *Manchester Guardian*, *The Observer* and *The Times* I could read online as a member of Manchester library. For Sellers at St Peter's School: *The Yorkshire Herald*, York library; and *The Peterite*, the school magazine, that you can read on the school's website, above all the 1923 and 1924 issues. The 1981 issue reprinted the *Yorkshire Post* obituary of Sellers by Kilburn. Through appeals in Yorkshire newspapers I was glad to hear from several people, notably Sellers' daughter-in-law Anne.

I thank also Stephen Chalke, for putting me on to Ron Deaton, who put me on to Andrew Sellers and Bryan Stott; David Moore, for his hospitality and letting me go through his volumes of *The Cricketer*; Neil Robinson in the library at Lord's for letting me see MCC papers; Peter Wynne-Thomas, librarian at Trent Bridge; and the Library and Museum of Freemasonry in Great Queen Street, London, free and well worth a visit, even for non-masons. I should add I have never been a Freemason nor ever wanted to be one.

I went through various Yorkshire club committee minutes at West Yorkshire council archives at Morley, file Wyl 2053; including an important memoir of Sellers by Ted Lester, in *White Rose* magazine, February 1990, which Ron Deaton told me about. Thanks also to Ron for a close read of this text; and for some of the 1930s and 1940s photographs. Others are from Roger Mann and William Roberts.

Dr Neil Carter of De Montfort University let me give a paper on Sellers on 29 January 2016, during my master's degree in sports history and culture; and Prof Dil Porter gave me the tip afterwards that the cricketing controversy between Sellers and Hammond in Australia in 1946 may have been personal.

The website *cricketarchive.com* was as ever useful for match and player records; my thanks to its then organiser Peter Griffiths; and to Mick Pope, for confirming to me at the March 2015 annual meeting of the Association of Cricket Statisticians and Historians in Derby that Sellers did not have a biographer. For details of sources by chapter, see online at markrowe. wordpress.com. The title of chapter three comes from the early Auden poem *Missing*; that and *In Memory of WB Yeats* are in his Collected Shorter

Thanks and Sources

Poems 1927-57.

My thanks to fellow ACS volunteers, editor Ray Greenall, who kindly made the statistical appendix; and proof-reader Kit Bartlett.

It only remains to offer what I thought aloud as I parted from Sidney Fielden. At the time, it felt profound: 'It's not the cricket; it's the people.'

Appendix
Some Statistics

First-Class Cricket: Batting and Fielding

	M	I	NO	R	HS	Ave	100	50	Ct
1932 (England)	29	37	5	804	85	25.12	0	6	14
1933 (England)	35	44	6	716	58	18.84	0	1	32
1934 (England)	36	49	4	1050	104	23.33	1	4	39
1935 (England)	36	47	3	885	80	20.11	0	6	31
1936 (England)	36	47	5	788	204	18.76	1	0	34
1937 (England)	32	45	6	868	109	22.25	2	1	29
1938 (England)	37	48	6	1143	93*	27.21	0	5	28
1939 (England)	33	38	3	708	63	20.22	0	3	19
1945 (England)	3	4	1	79	39	26.33	0	0	2
1946 (England)	29	40	8	1060	85*	33.12	0	10	24
1947 (England)	24	38	3	773	92	22.08	0	6	14
1948 (England)	14	18	3	396	91	26.40	0	3	7
Totals	**344**	**455**	**53**	**9270**	**204**	**23.05**	**4**	**45**	**273**
For Yorkshire	*334*	*437*	*51*	*8949*	*204*	*23.18*	*4*	*44*	*264*

Notes: Sellers was dismissed 188 times caught (47%), 120 times bowled (30%), 67 times lbw (17%), 14 times stumped (3%), 12 times run out (3%) and one time hit wicket. The bowlers who took his wicket most were: T.W.J.Goddard 13 times, F.R.Brown 12 times, G.A.E.Paine seven times and D.E.Davies, R.Howorth, R.A.Sinfield, H.A.Smith, T.P.B.Smith, M.W.Tate and L.J.Todd six times.

First-Class Centuries (4)

Score	For	Opponent	Venue	Season
104	Yorkshire[1]	The Australians	Sheffield	1934
204	Yorkshire[1]	Cambridge University	Fenner's	1936
109	Yorkshire[1]	Kent	Bradford	1937
103*	Yorkshire[1]	Nottinghamshire	Trent Bridge	1937

Note: The superscript [1] or [2] above in this and following tables denotes first or second innings

Some Statistics

First-Class Cricket: Bowling

	B	M	R	W	BB	Ave	5wi	10wm
1932 (England)	23	0	23	1	1-23	23.00	0	0
1933 (England)	356	11	200	4	2-10	50.00	0	0
1934 (England)	78	1	51	1	1-3	51.00	0	0
1935 (England)	18	1	8	0				
1936 (England)	342	12	194	1	1-44	194.00	0	0
1937 (England)	120	3	42	0				
1938 (England)	54	0	49	1	1-23	49.00	0	0
1939 (England)	58	1	31	0				
1945 (England)	24	0	17	0				
1946 (England)	12	2	0	0				
1947 (England)	108	5	48	0				
1948 (England)	20	0	13	1	1-0	13.00	0	0
Totals	**1213**	**36**	**676**	**9**	**2-10**	**75.11**	**0**	**0**
For Yorkshire	1195	6	653	8	2-10	81.62	0	0

Note: Of Sellers' nine First-Class wickets, three were bowled, four were caught, one was lbw and one was stumped. The batsman Sellers dismissed the most was G.Brown, twice.

152

Index

Counties
Cumberland 60
Derbyshire 8, 24, 43, 45, 46, 52, 131
Essex 57, 93, 96
Glamorgan 69, 93, 97, 107, 112
Gloucestershire 24, 38, 40, 43-44, 48, 69, 91, 93, 95, 97, 131
Hampshire 9, 38, 48, 65, 95, 115
Kent 24, 45, 63, 69
Lancashire 9, 24, 48, 50, 76, 93, 94, 110, 115, 123
Leicestershire 23, 43, 56, 122, 140
Lincolnshire 138
Middlesex 24, 25, 26, 38, 39, 41, 44, 45, 48, 63, 68, 70, 73-74, 88, 91, 93, 95, 96
Northamptonshire 58, 131
Nottinghamshire 25, 38, 40, 45, 65-66, 78, 79, 93, 95, 105, 106
Somerset 93, 94, 102, 123
Surrey 9, 24, 25, 40, 46, 61, 68, 78, 93, 94, 105-106, 109, 137
Sussex 9, 25, 39, 42, 54, 78, 94
Warwickshire 39, 42, 46, 58, 63, 93, 94, 111, 117
Worcestershire 24, 25, 30, 39, 44, 58, 96

Adelaide 83
Aird, Ronnie 111, 112
Allen, Gubby 33, 70, 101, 103, 110, 111
Altham, Harry 110
Amateurism 109-111, 113, 144
Ames, Les 24, 71, 103
Anti-Aircraft Command 77
Appleyard, Bob 103
Arabs 101
Arlott, John 11, 35, 144
Armstrong, Norman 58
Auden, WH 146
Auschwitz 141
Australian Services 92

Baildon 115
Baildon Green 18
Bailey, Trevor 83, 96, 129, 135
Balloon Command 77
Baker, George 91
Bankfoot 18
Bapty, John 76
Barber, AT 28

Barber, BH 126
Barber, Wilf 23, 24, 28, 44, 49, 59, 61, 75, 94, 95, 139
Barlow, Eddie 131
Barnes, Phil 44
Barnett, Charles 31, 91
Barnoldswick 62
Bartlett, Hugh 65
Beckwithshaw 136
Bedser, Alec 77, 84, 111, 136
Bell, Leonard 115
Berrow's Worcester Journal 22, 38
Bingley 19, 87, 114, 143, 146
Binks, Jimmy 72
Bird, Dickie 34, 50, 51, 136, 139-140
Birmingham 89, 118
Birmingham Post 32, 46, 56, 58
Blackburn, Derek 110
BOAC flying boat 83
Booth, Arthur 26, 50-51, 93, 94, 95, 97
Bournemouth 9, 38, 68, 95
Bowes, Bill 22, 23, 25, 29-30, 32, 33, 38, 41, 45, 46, 49, 58, 66, 68, 80, 83, 86, 91, 92, 94, 95, 97, 111, 118, 119-120, 129, 134, 135, 137, 139
Bowley, Ted 39
Boycott, Geoffrey 56, 60, 112-113, 118, 121, 123, 126, 128, 129, 131, 134, 137, 143
Bradford 44, 48, 49, 54, 66, 76, 93, 94, 110, 114, 120, 130, 134
Bradford League 15, 17, 121
Bradford Park Avenue 19, 38
Bradford Telegraph and Argus 5, 43
Bradman, Don 31, 33, 46, 66, 78, 84-85, 88
Bramall Lane, Sheffield 24, 37, 39, 41, 63, 102, 103
Braund, Len 41
Brennan, Don 96, 97
Bridlington 138
Brisbane 85
Bristol 28, 43, 46, 91, 97, 117
Bristol Evening World 43, 44, 88, 91, 97
Brown, Freddie 37, 89, 103, 112, 131
Buckston, Robin 43
Buddenbrooks 14
Burnet, Ronnie 72, 102, 104-105, 106, 110, 111, 138, 140, 141
Butler, Harold 66
Byas, David 133, 134

153

Index

Cambridge 93
Cambridge News 39, 65
Cambridge University 7, 16, 53, 64
Canterbury 76
Cardiff 93
Cardus, Neville 50, 71, 73, 74, 77
Carr, Arthur 29, 38, 69
Carr, Donald 111
Cary, Cliff 86
Cassandra 106
Challenge match of 1937, 72-74
Chapman, Percy 69
Cherwell 5
Chesterfield 45, 46, 52, 63, 64, 93, 109
Clarke, Bertie 131
Clay, Johnny 63, 93
Close, Brian 25, 54, 58, 112, 114, 117, 118, 121, 122, 123, 124, 128, 129, 130, 131, 141, 143
Coates JG 43
Cobham, Lord 86
Cold War 47
Compton, Denis 44, 71, 75, 96
Conisborough 115
Constantine, Learie 62, 77, 88-89
Cooper, Eddie 30-31
Cope, Geoff 119, 124, 134, 135, 142, 145, 147
Cornford, Tich 58
Country Life magazine 72, 73
Cowdrey, Colin 33, 135-136
Coxon, Alec 54-55, 91, 92, 94, 97, 103
Cranfield, Monty 44
Cranmer, Peter 93
Crapp, Jack 38
Craven district 14
Craven Gentlemen 16
Crawford, Mike 110, 126
Cultural Revolution 127

Darling, William 14
Davies, Emrys 93
Dennis, Frank 61
Derby Evening Telegraph 46, 52, 63, 64, 109
Devonshire Hotel, Keighley 12
Dewsbury 12
D'Oliveria, Basil 137
Dollery, Tom 103
Dolphin, Arthur 81
Dolphin, Brian 136
Doncaster 110, 115
Dooland, Bruce 105
Duckworth, Leslie 28
Duckworth, TB 25, 45, 46

Eagar, Desmond 38
Eastbourne 95
Ebeling, Hans 66
Eckersley, Peter 50
Edgbaston 39, 42, 46, 56, 117
Edrich, Bill 41, 43, 45, 49, 70, 74, 77, 85, 86, 88, 96, 106

Eldwick 143
Elliott, Harry 64
Epsom 79
Evans, Godfrey 88
Evening Press, York 133
Express, Daily 86, 110, 115

Fender, Percy 9
Fiddling, Kenneth 131
Fielden, Sidney 35, 114, 115, 129
Fleetwood-Smith, Leslie 66
Freeman, Tich 63
Freemasonry 33-34, 137
Fry, CB 23, 28, 32

Ganton Golf Club 27
Gargrave 60
Garland-Wells, Monty 79
Gentlemen versus Players 37, 70-71, 115, 135
Gibb, Paul 23, 25, 44, 93
Gibson, Alan 118
Gillette Cup 112, 113, 123
Gilligan, Arthur 117
Glasgow 91
Glusburn 21
Goddard, Tom 34, 71
Gordon, Sir Home 31, 68, 69
Grace, WG 117
Grand Hotel, Scarborough 135
Graveney, Tom 90, 91, 97
Green Howards 76
Greenwood, Frank 19, 20
Grimmett, Clarrie 66
Guardian, The 124, 125, 144

Hall, Charles 30, 68
Hammond, Walter 24, 29, 33, 38, 41, 48, 57, 71, 74, 78, 84, 85-86, 87, 90, 93, 107, 114, 134, 135
Hampshire, John 54, 128, 129, 130, 132, 137
Harbord, WE 20
Hardstaff, Joe 71
Harewood, Earl of 33
Harris, Bruce 94
Harris, Charles 79
Harrogate 62, 89, 97, 136
Harrow School 81
Harvey, Fred 5
Hastilow, CAF 111, 112
Hawke, Lord 12, 24, 41-42, 45, 48, 58, 68, 73, 79, 104, 117, 130, 135
Headingley 27, 50, 68, 74, 75, 93, 95, 97, 112, 116, 122, 139
Heane, George 78, 93
Hearne, Jack 7, 12
Hendren, Patsy 73
Henley, Herbert 9
Hesketh, Clifford 103, 104
Heyhirst, Bright 6, 25, 80, 93
Hirst, George 18, 109
Hobbs, Jack 28, 29

154

Index

Hodgson, Derek 128
Hodgson, Frank 50
Hollies, Eric 63
Holmes, AJ 30, 78, 86
Holmes, Errol 37, 61, 78, 112
Holmes, Percy 5, 81, 120
Home, Alec Douglas 118
Hove 57, 58, 64, 109
Hovingham Hall 101
Howard, Geoffrey 110
Huddersfield 109
Hull 39, 97, 124
Hutton, Len 10, 23, 25, 32-33, 37-38, 49, 53, 56, 71, 75, 80, 85, 93, 94, 95, 97, 105, 113, 115, 128, 135, 136, 138, 139, 142
Hutton, Richard 128

Iddon, Jack 49, 50
Ikin, Jack 84, 85
Ilkley 147
Illingworth, Raymond 72, 108, 116, 117, 119-120, 121-122, 126, 128, 130, 137
India 24, 86, 93-94, 142
Ingrow, Keighley 15
Insole, Doug 103, 112
Isis 5

Jackson, Guy 8
Jackson, Sir Stanley 31, 78, 86, 88
Jamaica 29
James, CLR 30, 66
Jardine, Douglas 29, 33
Johnson, Joseph 25
Jowett van 89

Keeton, Walter 45, 77
Keighley 133
Keighley Cricket Club 12
Keighley Golf Club 14
Keighley News 12, 19, 20, 21
Kilburn, JM 19, 23, 24, 30, 39, 43, 49, 55, 57, 58-59, 63, 75, 88, 92, 93, 94, 95, 97, 125, 126, 127, 139, 144
Kilner, Norman 39, 81
King, Phil 25
Kyle, Duncan 66

Laker, Jim 75, 106
Langridge, James 84
Langridge, John 39, 45
Larwood, Harold 41, 65
Lawkholme, Keighley 14, 19
Lawkholme Lane 18, 130
Leadbeater, Eddie 63
Lee, Frank 38
Leeds 123, 130
Leeds Medical School 146
Leese, Oliver 118
Leicester 39, 41, 52, 58, 94
Leicester Evening Mail 47, 52
Leicester Mercury 29, 52
Lester, Ted 51, 133, 138

Leveson-Gower, Sir Henry 27, 92
Lewis, Tony 136
Leyland, Maurice 6, 10, 11, 23, 25, 27, 34, 46, 49, 50, 74, 75, 77, 78, 80, 81, 93, 94, 95, 134, 139
Leyton 68
Lindwall, Ray 40, 45
Lister, Dorothy 87
Lister, Lionel 123, 124
Little John, 59, 95, 96
London Evening News 24, 29
London Evening Standard 7, 23, 94
Longrigg, Bunty 93
Lord's 7, 8, 25, 28, 30, 38, 39, 44, 45, 63, 70, 77, 78, 79, 86, 92, 93, 96, 107, 109, 110, 112, 134, 139
Lowson, Frank 103
Lupton, Major AW 19
Lyon, Bev 69
Lyon, MD 77

Macaulay, George 5, 10, 19, 39, 50, 61, 68, 81
Mail, Daily 49, 102, 103, 104, 108, 117
Mailey, Arthur 28
Mallalieu. JPW 6
Manchester 63, 68, 92
Manchester Guardian 50, 66, 71
Manchester United 115
Mao Tse-tung 127
Marshall, Howard 28, 71
Martin, Sidney 44
May, Peter 103, 110
MCC 7, 30, 38, 63, 78, 83, 84, 85, 88, 89, 95, 101, 102, 103, 111, 117, 118, 121, 146
MCC inquiry 109, 111
Melbourne 85
Melbourne Cup 83
Melville, Alan 5, 8, 52
Mewies, Jack 123, 125-126, 130
Mirror, Daily 106, 108, 123
Mitchell, Arthur 6, 23, 29, 38, 42, 47, 59, 74, 75, 126, 134, 139
Mitchell, Tommy 63, 64
Mitchell-Innes, Norman 70
Moscow Olympics 119
Mosey, Don 89, 139
Moss, Stirling 114
Moyes, AG 37, 52

Nash, Jack 21, 54, 107, 120, 122, 124, 126, 141
New Zealanders 46, 68, 70
Nicknames 59
Norfolk, Duke of 110, 112
Northampton 41, 53
Northampton Chronicle and Echo 28
Northern Cricket Society 121
Northern Echo 133
Nottingham Evening News 27
Nottingham Journal 41, 42, 45, 65
Nourse, Dudley 37

155

Index

Old Trafford, Manchester 49, 94, 142
Oval, The 9, 23, 29, 46, 63, 94, 105, 117
Owen-Smith, Tuppy 5, 6, 46, 63, 73
Oxford 57
Oxford Mail 5, 32, 53, 93
Oxford University 5

Padgett, Doug 117, 126, 128
Paine, George 32, 63
Parker, Jack 77
Parks, Jim 57
Parks, The 5
Pearce, TN 77, 93
Peebles, Ian 135
Peel, Bobby 12
Perks, Reg 44, 45
Peter's, St, York school 16
Pettiford, Jack 92
Pike, Horace 115
Plaindealer 8
Poaching of Yorkshire players 120-121
Pollard, Dick 84
Poole harbour 83
Priestley Cup 19
Procter, Mike 131
Pudsey 10, 32, 134
Pudsey St Lawrence 19
Punch magazine 46

Quaife, Bernard 44
Queensbury 17

Rait Kerr, RS 88, 110
Rangoon 83
Ranji 33
Redcar 19
Richardson, Arthur 45
Ringrose, William 61, 80
Rhodes, Arthur 7, 48, 61, 68
Rhodes, Wilfred 8, 81, 114, 117, 118
Rhodesia 119
Riddington, Tony 39
Robertson-Glasgow, RC 7, 38, 63, 70, 77-78, 91
Robins, Walter 26, 38, 40, 45, 63, 70, 71, 72, 78, 86, 93, 111, 112
Robinson, Ellis 25, 34-35, 58, 60, 65, 93, 94, 95, 115
Root, Joe 133
Rose Bay, Sydney 83
Ross, Alan 129
Rostron, Frank 110
Rotherham 19
Royal Australian Air Force 92

Saltaire 12, 61
Savoy, London 46
Scarborough 24, 58, 63, 83, 92, 95, 135
Scarborough Festival 27, 37
Scott, Robert 21
Sellers, Andrew (Brian's son) 14, 17, 38, 71, 88, 89, 127, 132, 134, 146, 147
Sellers. Anne (Brian's daughter-in-law) 61, 115-116
Sellers, Arthur (Brian's father) 9, 12, 14, 15, 16, 49, 71
Sellers, Brian 5-10, 14, 16; playing for Keighley 17-19; becoming Yorkshire captain 19-21; given Yorkshire cap 21-22; player 23-27; golfer, 27; and Sutcliffe 27-29; and Bowes 29-30; and Verity 30-31; and Hutton 31-32; not a Freemason 33-34; and Ellis Robinson 34-35; on the field 37-53; in Australia 43, 45, 83-89, 139; off the field 54-61, 133-134; return from Australia 59, 83; and Boycott 60-61, 128-129, 130, 131; wedding 61; as batsman 62-66; as fielder, 66, 68; as bowler 68; as captain 68-71, 133-134, 135, 137-138; business 71-72; England selector 74; war service 77; Wisden cricketer of the year 77-78; MCC committee work 78; criticism of Hammond 85-86, 90; postwar player 91-100; as wicket-keeper 93, 96-97; as committee man 101, 103, 109-132, 138, 139-140, 142, 144, 145; and Wardle 102-108; swearing 104, 105, 113, 115, 136-137, 142; and Close 114-115, 121, 122, 123, 128-129, 131; and Illingworth 119-120, 121-122; and Geoff Cope 134-135; and Colin Cowdrey 135-136; death 144, 146; obituaries of 144; memorabilia auctioned 147.
Sellers, Bright (Brian's wife) 61, 143
Sellers, David (Brian's son) 17, 147
Sellers, Godfrey (Brian's brother) 16, 126, 128
Sellers, Herbert 17, 33
Sellers, Mary (Brian's mother) 14, 16
Sellers, Robert (Arthur's father) 14
Shackleton, Allan 18
Sharpe, Phil 128
Sheffield 12, 37, 48, 49, 52, 66, 73, 93, 94, 95, 123, 127
Sheffield Telegraph 25, 30, 40, 57, 63, 70, 93
Sherwood Foresters 29
Shipley 115
Sims, Jim 63
Singapore 83
Skipton 123, 130
Smailes, Frank 7, 23, 33, 49, 65, 66, 68, 77, 94, 95, 97
Smith, Jim 39
Smith, Ray 96
Smithson, Gerald 97
Sobers, Garry 132
Sock-snipping 133
South Africa 74
Spion Kop, Sheffield 48
Sprotborough 24
Stalin 55, 141
Stanley, John 105
Statham, Brian 115

156

Stevens, Greville 48
Stott, Bryan 33, 114, 116, 117, 129, 130, 136, 141, 145
Stourbridge 38, 39
Sunday League 114, 124, 129
Surridge, Stuart 105-106, 137
Sussex Daily News 8, 9, 30, 42, 64
Sutcliffe, Billy 102
Sutcliffe, Herbert 5, 10, 19, 23, 25, 27-29, 32, 34, 46, 53, 56, 64, 68, 75, 108, 109, 119, 124, 126, 139
Swanton, EW 23, 29, 35, 46, 101, 103, 106, 109, 135, 143
Sydney Harbour Bridge 83
Symond, Ronald 49

Tate, Maurice 64
Taunton 38, 94, 117, 141
Telegraph, Daily 28, 71, 103
Temple, John 134
Tendulkar, Sachin 132
Times, The 40, 44, 49, 68, 71, 92, 109, 111, 117, 118, 126
Todd, Eric 125, 126
Tompkin, Maurice 39
Toyne, Stanley 65
Trent Bridge 95, 97
Troth, Steve 117, 130
Trueman, Arthur 142
Trueman, Fred 10, 79, 101, 106, 114, 115, 117, 129, 137, 141-142, 145
Turnbull, Maurice 69, 78
Turner, Cyril 28, 33, 34, 66, 68, 75, 77, 94, 139

Ulyatt, Richard 123
Ulyett, George 12

Valentine, Bryan 69, 86
Verity, Hedley 6, 23, 25, 30-31, 32, 39, 43, 45, 46, 50, 53, 65, 68, 76, 91, 115, 117, 118, 139
Voce, Bill 26, 41, 45, 65, 84

Wakefield 139
Wall, Tim 66

Walters, Cyril 69
Wardle, Johnny 14, 24, 54, 55, 58, 75, 91-92, 97, 100, 101, 102-108, 117, 120, 121, 122, 123, 138, 142-143
Warne, Frank 44
Warner, Sir Pelham 86
Washbrook, Cyril 75
Watch, Will 95
Watson, Willie 51, 56, 75, 91, 97, 117, 137
Wellings, EM 24, 31, 112, 139
West Indies 62, 68, 109
White, Crawford 115
Wilcox, Denys 37
Wilson, Don 128, 146
Wilson, Geoffrey 81
Wilson, Vic 110, 112, 117, 140
Wood, Arthur 6, 23, 34, 45, 59, 61, 65, 66, 75, 139
Woodcock, John 117, 126
Woodford, John 124
Wooller, Wilf 64, 103, 107, 108, 112
Woolley, Frank 12, 70, 78
Worcester 24, 33, 45
Worcester Evening News 45
Worker, Daily 32, 135
Worsley, Sir William 101, 124, 125, 126, 129, 141
Wright, Doug 63, 77, 84, 88
Wyatt, Bob 56, 66, 69, 70, 78
Wyke 14

Yardley, Norman 16-17, 23, 26, 31, 33, 34, 53, 54, 58, 64, 70, 75, 82, 85, 88, 89, 91, 95, 97, 102, 103, 104, 106, 107, 126, 135, 138
Yeats, WB 146
Yorkdale Press 71
Yorkshire Cricket Council 12
Yorkshire Evening News 5, 83
Yorkshire Evening Post 57, 59, 83, 84, 95, 96
Yorkshire Gazette & Herald 133
Yorkshire Post 6, 20, 21, 32, 39, 68, 73, 120, 123, 125, 126, 133, 142
Yorkshire Society 24